Sheila M. Amari
3/21/18

BIPOLAR DAD. BORDERLINE HUSBAND

Sheila M. Amari

LifeRich Publishing is a registered trademark of
The Reader's Digest Association, Inc.

LifeRich Publishing books may be ordered through booksellers or by contacting:

LifeRich Publishing
1663 Liberty Drive
Bloomington, IN 47403
www.liferichpublishing.com
1 (888) 238-8637

Because of the dynamic nature of the Internet, any web addresses or
links contained in this book may have changed since publication and
may no longer be valid. The views expressed in this work are solely those
of the author and do not necessarily reflect the views of the publisher,
and the publisher hereby disclaims any responsibility for them.

Any people depicted in stock imagery provided by Thinkstock are models,
and such images are being used for illustrative purposes only.
Certain stock imagery © Thinkstock.

ISBN: 978-1-4897-1163-2 (sc)
ISBN: 978-1-4897-1162-5 (e)

Library of Congress Control Number: 2017933765

Print information available on the last page.

LifeRich Publishing rev. date: 5/15/2017

CONTENTS

DEDICATION

This book is dedicated to everyone who has been abused spiritually, mentally, verbally, or physically. It is to awaken people who have personality disorders, and behavioral problems; to inspire them to try hard to be less selfish, and become aware of what their relationship means to their families. It is to encourage dysfunctional families to work at living in peace and treating each other with respect.

Praise God for those who have found Grace, and been able to overcome their abuse. To those who are searching for help, my prayer is that you will find the only "WAY"...Jesus Christ and partake of his joy, and peace. If and when you do, please pass the "GOOD NEWS" on to others in need.

Luke 1:31, I John 5:4-5

Author: Sheila M. Amari

ABBREVIATION

Scriptures are taken from King James Version (KIV) of the Bible.

Names of the books in the Bible, used in this book, may be abbreviated, using the first two-four letters of the book name.

Pphd = Paraphrased

Ill = illustration

Pic = Pictures

Chapter	SCRIPTURE
1	Isa. 49:1, 5
2	Dt. 20:12
3	I Jn. 4:18
4	Psa. 15:6
5	Pa. 5:3
6	Jam. 3:14
7	Act. 20:27
8	Jam. 1:12
9	Psa. 103:2

ACKNOWLEDGEMENT

Those who have worked at the Publisher's Office to help, guide, and advise me, have been a joy to work with. I greatly appreciate their patience and kindness. They have taught me that my computer can do things, which I did not know it could do.

God Almighty I acknowledge, for giving to me the ability to write this book. He is my source, strength, joy, and peace. All that I am and all that I have, I give back to him. Praise God for His mercy and grace. I love HIM with all my heart.

Author: Sheila M. Amari

INTRODUCTION

This book will peak curiosity and stir emotions. Written in the third person, it is about a girl who was abused verbally, mentally, and physically by her dad and her husband. They both treated her like she was their slave.

Some events are based on truth, and names have been changed. Others are embellished to obscure the truth. Parts are fiction to stir the emotions, and hold the reader's attention.

She was born with a heart problem and the doctors told her parents, that she would not live, when she was born. Her parents abandoned her for five years. During that time she lived with her grandparents. Later, she was held back, by her parents, when it came to normal childhood activities, but forced to work like a man, on the farm, and a maid, in the house.

Her husband moved her around, within five states. He traveled on his job, and was gone more than half of the time, leaving her to raise two boys, maintain the household, do yard work, take care of all business, and make most decisions related to their family, while living away from relatives and friends.

Author: Sheila M. Amari

CHAPTER ONE

BORN TO DIE

Isaiah 49: 1, 5: The Lord formed me from the womb. KJV

It was a brisk afternoon in December. Ruth yelled to five-year-old Ryle. "Start a fire in the kitchen, wood stove, and put on a pot of water to boil." "Why, mama? What for, mama?" Just do what I say and you stay in the kitchen", she yelled back. Ruth had birthed twelve children of her own, and now was about to deliver her first grandchild.

Cassie, next to oldest of twelve children, was in labor for long hours, and her husband Frank, eventually decided Ruth needed help, if Cassie and the baby were to live. Therefore, he scampered to bring in two medical doctors, to help Ruth finish the task.

In early morning, Beulah Rose Shiloam weighed in at six pounds, eighteen inches long and had blue eyes. She was the first of six children. The difficult birth caused by the prolonged labor, caused pressure on her head against Cassie's pelvic bone. It caused a swelling, like an upside down cone, on top of her head. She had heart problems, and the doctors told her parents that she would not live. Cassie was a long time recovering. The doctors told her that she was not built for having babies, and that she should not have any more children. It is something most people do not think about, that everyone is dying from the minute they are born. Imagine what it is like to EXPECT to die every minute you are living. Beulah was born December 1933 with Mitral Valve Prolapse. All her life she had weak spells and shortness of breath. She stumbled around a lot. Tomorrow is not a given.

As a toddler, pictures and tales by relative confirmed that it took about a year for the cone shape to dissipate, from Beulah's head. Her parents would never talk about it or tell her why doctors said she would not live. They would not let her do things which her peers did. The family feared she might have brain damage and they always treated her differently. Her parents always told people that it was her nerves, when she had a weak spell. One day, at the dinner table, when she was a teenager, Frank tried to tell her why the doctors said she would not live, when she was born. When he got to the main point, he looked at Cassie and said "you tell her". That was the end of that conversation.

Frank named Beulah, after his teenage girl friend (Beulah). He wanted to marry her, but she would not have anything to do with him. The middle name Rose was for his sister Rose. He was third of seven boys in his family, then, Rose was the first of three girls - totaling ten children in his family.

After Cassie was recovered enough to travel, she and Frank: moved, in the A Model Ford, forty miles across the local river, to Moose County Georgia,and left Beulah with her maternal grandparents (the Woodall's) until she was age five. During those years her parents lived with his parents and farmed. They visited on a few weekends. There was no bonding between them and her. They fussed at her for walking around, holding her hands crossed over her private parts, telling her to move her hands. She had very few memories of her parents, during the five years she lived there.

D.J. and Ruth Woodall were first cousins. Their parents

arranged their marriage, when she was age thirteen and he was age twenty-one. Bearing five girls and seven boys Ruth delivered them each at home alone. She said she spreaded a quilt on the floor, got down on her hands and knees, and had each baby. She had one set of twin boys.

They both were descendants of "Cherokee Indians" and he was a descendent of Robert E. Lee. His grandmother Ester was full blooded Cherokee. He was short, chubby and sweet. He hardly ever spoke, but smiled a lot. She had beautiful red hair, which she wore up in a bun, until he died. She had it cut short and had a permanent put in for the rest of her life, which was the style at that time. The daughters influenced that.

Ruth and D.J.'s oldest child died as a toddler, before the others were born. They drove a wagon loaded with vegetables, pulled by one old skinny, red mule, headed for the market. May, a beautiful curly, blond-haired girl, put a Sweet Pea in her mouth, and sucked it down her throat. Saving her was impossible.

D. J. walked their first and only milk cow about 68 miles, within three days, to their home in Sartain, S. C., from Lando, GA. The reason they thought they needed a milk cow, was because Frank: (being the controlling person that he was) convinced them that they needed one. He also convinced the twin boys to go to the dentist and have each of their front tusks pulled, so, as an adult, their teeth would grow straight.

The Woodall family was humble, quite, poor, and Godly people. They were law- abiding citizens, and not proud people. There was no knowledge of them getting into trouble, of any sort. There were no memories of ever hearing of a fuss, or disagreement between any of them. They worked hard, and respected everyone.

Cassie and Frank was a nice looking couple. She was dark skinned (Cherokee Indian), 5'2" tall, had beautiful, dark, silky hair, which Beulah liked to comb, and had a good figure. Frank was 5'11" tall, had red hair, was fair skinned, and was very handsome.

Grandpa D.J. use to come home from the mill, in the afternoons, and get Beulah a piece of fatback out of the oven. He and she would go sit on the front porch, in their straight back chairs. As he chewed his tobacco, they just smiled at each other. He was not a talker. Watching the sun go down, they waited, for Ruth to come walking home from work. They worked different shifts. He had a "Wen" (Sebaceous Cyst, which grew no hair) on the top, left side of his head, about the size of a nickel in diameter, and about one forth inch deep. Beulah use to stare at it when sitting on the porch.

They sat Beulah down in a straight chair, by the small, Franklin, Coal heater, in the dark, corner of the dining room, which had the shade pulled, while everyone went to work and school. Cassie claimed that there was always someone asleep in the large, back room, but Beulah does not remember such. There was a door to the room off the back porch where the boys came after shift work and slept during some day hours. It had three double beds. Beulah was not allowed to go in there at any time. She did peek into it several times. There were clothes strewn around the room. The adults worked at the Cotton mill, about a block away, and the boys walked to school.

CRISIS! Bang! Crash! Screaming! Beulah hears two cars crash outside the window, just six feet from the house. She was so afraid. They had told her not to get up, out of the chair, nor go to the window. The shade was always pulled down over the only window in the dining room where she sat, while they were all gone to work and school. When she needed to go to the toilet, which was located on the back porch, but was not allowed to go alone, she had to wait until someone came home to escort her, to the toilet. Grandma Ruth or one of the girls carried her to the restroom at lunchtime, suppertime and bedtime.

There were three things that Beulah feared. Sitting alone in that dark room, fearing the high back steps, and the day Frank took her away from her grandparents.

For the first year Ruth chewed up Green Beans and other vegetables, and put them in Beulah's mouth, to get her to eat, when she was an infant. Later, they turned a chair around and stood her on her knees, at the table, at meal times. Ryle and the boys use to tease her at the table. When Frank was there, he made them stop. He told them not to give her candy or sweets. Beulah would ask Ruth for a "Vanilla Wafer". Cassie would say "no" she cannot have a "Vanilla Wafer", but Ruth would hand her one (repeatedly) each time she asked, even in Cassie's presence. Beulah bonded with her grandma Ruth, not with her mama, Cassie. She also bonded with her grandpa D. J. and not her daddy Frank.

Cassie's family did not approve of her marriage to Frank, because he was an Alcoholic. Once she left him and moved back home with her parents. After going back with him, she said she would never leave him again. She asked him to promise that he would quit drinking. He told her "I will make you one promise, that you will never see me drunk again". From then on, he always stayed away when he drank, except for his usual substantial snorts, when he walked in the door, at meal time. Her family put him down. Each time she got pregnant her sisters got in a big uproar, about how awful he was.

The five room mill hill houses where Beulah lived with her grandparents, four aunts, and seven uncles (one set of twin uncles), was on the comer of Eighth Street. The house was typical for a mill hill. It had a front and back porch, and a rest room on the back porch.

Entering the front porch, then the front door was her grandparent's bedroom. It had two standard beds, a small table between, under the window, and one chest of-drawers. Left was Cassie's room where she claimed Frank slept during the day and worked third shift, in the Cotton Mill. However, Beulah remembers they were separated for some time. Her third sister Farris was born while there. She can remember sleeping on a Mohair sofa, in front of the fireplace. She slept on one end of the sofa and Drusie slept on the other end. Baby Farris slept in a crib. The double bed was turned comer wise. The room was extremely crowded. The fireplace was closed.

Going from the grandparent's room (living room), was the small kitchen, which had a wood stove, sink, and one small cabinet. Grandma Ruth use to make the best sawmill gravy, using cornmeal instead of flour. Beulah never knew anyone else who could make it. She made delicious pickled green beans, in a chum like making Sour Crout.

Left was the dining room. There was a 5' long table in the middle of the room, between where she sat and the one window, with the shade pulled down. Twelve straight back chairs (which D.J. had bottomed) surrounded the table. There was one Franklin, Coal heater, and the Coal bucket (in the comer). Beulah's chair was between the kitchen door, and the heater. There was a Singer, peddle, sewing machine at the left wall of the room, and a China, dish cabinet next to the right wall. That is all that was in the room, except one picture of two mountains, with a train entering the center, between the two mountains. *Beulah never heard of the word "toy", or "book".* No one ever read or told her a story. She never had any play mates, or children friends her age. Only time she went outside, was with her parents or relatives when they came on holidays.

Off the kitchen was a narrow back porch, which had a

bathroom, to the left. It only had a commode, a shower, and one sink. There were high back steps. She was not allowed to go to the bathroom, until someone came home and went with her. So, she sat with nothing to do. She never had any toys. She never heard the word toys. Sometimes the street sounds were scary. But she was told to not get out of the chair, or peek past the shade.

The boy's room had a door entrance from the back porch. Therefore, when they returned home from school or shift work, they did not come through the house. Beulah did not see them. There was usually someone sleeping, during the day, somewhere in the house She had very few memories of her parents during the five years she lived there.

Great grandpa Travis Shaw came on one or more occasions, during the winter months, for a week. He sat in her chair and held her on his knees. He was "Club Footed" in both feet. They were each drawn up in a ball. He made his own shoes out of Prince Albert metal cans, for the souls, and dried animal skins (which he had dried) for the upper part of each shoe. He was a sweet, frail, tall, red-curly headed man.

Beulah's extended family walked her to church regularly, at Wither's Baptist Church, a block away. Cassie said that, before she married she had to turn over her pay check to her mama, and she convinced her, to allow her to keep ten cents, from each pay check for the tithe.

∞

While living in Georgia with his parents, it was there their second child, Drusie, was born sixteen months after Beulah. She was a ten-pound, beautiful, brown eyed baby and posed no problems in birthing. Drusie always had to have her way. One time Frank, Cassie and Drusie came to visit. They were making Drusie and Beulah's pictures together on the front porch. Beulah had the empty camera box. However, Drusie decided she wanted it. Frank made Beulah give it to Drusie. That was the story of Beulah's whole life, while growing up. Frank would tell Beulah "now, she is the youngest, let her have it". That was the only way to shut her up. This was a pattern of Beulah's parent's treatment of her. Beulah would not take a bottle nor drink milk, anymore. Growing up, her dad would plead with her to drink buttermilk with him, which on occasions she would give in. There was one occasion, when Frank and Bessie visited; he carried Drusie and Beulah to the fairground. He had their picture made with him holding them, one in each arm, wearing little sailor caps, which he had bought for them. Farris, Beulah's second sister was born about three years later. Cassie came to the hospital in Sartain, SC for the birth. .

About 1:00pm, on a hot Saturday, July afternoon, Cassie's relatives were at the Pentecostal Holiness Tent Revival, on Eighth street, about a block from their residence, when Frank, Cassie, and Beulah's two siblings came, to move her away. She felt the Holy Spirit for the first time in her life. She was determined not to leave. Aunt Chrystal gave her an expensive gold ring with a large green set, from her finger, to get her to go, and told her to wear it until she got married. Then, she was to return it, which she did. When Chrystal died, Beulah was to inherit the ring. However, a cousin got it, and Beulah never told her that she was to get the ring. Frank had to literally drag Beulah away and put her into the A model Ford.

∞

He moved them into an old, unpainted, rundown one-room shack, in the edge of the swamp water, in Loreal, S.C, about a mile from where her maternal grandparents lived. It was there that her third sibling, brother Saul was born, a few months later.

There was only one double bed, one chest of drawers, and a pallet, which the three girls slept on, in that one room house. It did have a back door which went out onto a small 4' x 3' porch with banisters around it. The children were not allowed to go out there, because the swamp water came up part of the way on the foundation.

During the brief time they lived there, Frank continued to travel up north, with his car sales buddies, to pull down cars. One trip, he brought back a piano, loaded it into the opposite side of the room, from the bed, and said Beulah was going to learn to play it. Cassie had one year of piano training, and taught her to read the notes and time. That was the beginning of a lifetime of a gospel music ministry, for Beulah. She loved playing it and preferred playing by ear. That was inherited talent from Cassie's family. She did not have any music lessons.

A close friend of the family about Drusie's age was run over by a car, just up the street from their house. She was injured critically, and crippled for life. It took years for her to recover enough to function.

One afternoon Beulah saw a woman thrown out of a large truck, which had the passenger door tom off, as it slung a curve, at the intersection almost in front of their house. It was a very rough neighborhood.

Cassie's family was musicians. The twins Marion Holt and Harold Colt played the accordion, guitar, etc. Joshua played any string instrument he could get his hands on. He was manager of two different Radio Stations, and owned his own station in Georgia for years, as an adult.

∞

After six months there, Frank moved them across the river, into Moose County, Georgia. He had purchased a 150 year old house, on a dirt road, and twenty-five acres of farm land. Not long after moving there, he built a large kitchen, and a wrap-a-round back porch, on the back of the house. Each room was 15' x 18'. It was originally two rooms; a living room and a bedroom. They had two double beds, in the same room, where Frank, Cassie, and the baby slept in one and the three girls slept in the other one. Later, there was a cot for their brother Saul. The family of eight lived there until the first grandson was born.

The weather in north Georgia was always a few degrees cooler than in Alabama or Mississippi. The high ranged from around 102 – 50 degrees in the summer, and the low ranged from around 60 – minus 2 in the winter.

Frank had four large barns. The last one he built was two stories. Beulah begged Cassie to all move into it, while Frank was gone. It was nicer was about two-hundred years old. However, they were afraid to do it. Beulah use to say, that Frank cared more about his cattle than he did the family. Drusie and Beulah always slept in the same bed. Farris and Millie slept in one bed. Saul slept on a cot, and Todd slept in the baby bed.

They raised six children in this small, three room house. When the two oldest girls became teens, they moved their double bed into the living room, where the piano was. As the next two children came alone, they slept on a small cot in their parent's room. Eventually, Frank took in the rap-a-round back porch, on the west end, and made a small bedroom for the two younger girls.

Beulah was use to her aunts, uncles, and grandparents doting over her. After she was moved away from them, no one ever doted over her, or showed her any affection. Her parents never told her that they loved her, except Frank would say "this is for your good, or we are doing this because we love you," when he wanted her to do something she did not want to do. She cannot remember her parents ever holding her or sitting her on their lap, except the time where he had his picture made holding her and Drusie, at the Fairgrounds.

On a beautiful Sunday afternoon Uncle Reilly Shiloam came over in a new "A Model" Ford. He and Frank decided to ride and try it out. Of course, there was no small bit of objection from Aunt Tilley (Reilly's wife and Jewel's mother), and Cassie did not want them to go try out the new car. However, the men decided to let the girls go with them. The girls were about age seven, five, and four. After all they were too young to know much about what was going on. Therefore, Drusie, Jewel Shiloam and Beulah went with them. Reilly drove to Fortress, Georgia about eighty miles away to an old, unpainted two story house. They pulled in and parked in the yard. They all got out and went in. The house had a long, wide hall down the center. On the right were rooms of young girls fixing ladies hair. On the left were rooms with the doors closed. That is where the two men each went into separate rooms, after they placed each of the three girls in a different room, on the left side of the hall, with hair dressers, who doated over them, to have their hair combed. Beulah was old enough to remember this and never told anyone until after all four of the adults were deceased. She figured out, during those years, what Frank and Reilly were up to, that day.

She had to get used to using the slop jar and outhouse. At least on the mill hill they had running water and a commode. She had to get familiar with drawing water from the well, using the water bucket and dipper, the wash bowl to wash hands, and the soap dish.

She loved all of her Woodall relatives very much. There was nothing wicked or ignorant about any of them. A few did have mental deficiencies. They were obedient, and altruistic.

Regarding her siblings, Drusie was lazy, "Miss Beautiful", goody-goody, never feared punishment or cared about obeying.

Her second sister was "Miss Liberated", pretty, talented, smart, Miss Perfection, a work-a-holic, and Miss Permissive. The first brother was rebellious, and defiant. The third sister was the one with the terrible temper. She and Frank could never get along. Her baby brother was humble, Phlegmatic, and the sweetest of them all. Frank would not let the last three go with the Trio to sing, except when the whole family went. They did not have a singing voice. Frank worked Todd like he was a slave, and talked to him like he was a dog. Todd just kept taking it, until his wife and Beulah taught him how to stand up to Frank.

Frank only went through the eighth grade. He loved to brag about; he won a writing contest in school "for such pretty penmanship". When traveling, he took pride in pointing out where farms had barns. He would say "you can tell who is the boss of that place", and smiled real big. One day in the summer time, three of Franks barns burned down at the same time (including the new, two story), and no one ever knew what started the fires.

In the second grade, one day the teacher asked what each child would like to be, when they grew- up. Beulah held up her hand and said that "she wanted to be a farmer and raise kids".

Beulah wore brown, leather high top shoes to school, which was the only pair she had. Parents bought shoes a little too large, so the children could grow into them and wear them longer. School had recently started back in the fall, and she was in the second grade. She could not find a pair of socks in the sock drawer. Therefore, she wore the shoes to school without socks, and they rubbed her leg. She came home with her left leg red, swollen, and sore from her ankle to her knee. They carried her to the doctor, who said that she had Aircyphlis in her left leg. She had to sit, soaking her foot and leg in a bucket of salt water every night, for an hour, over a period of weeks.

It was during the fourth grade, that one girl decided the other girls needed to learn about sex and that she was the one to do it. It was their strong quest to learn about sex that caused the girls to give control over to her, so they consented. She and her cousin, neighbor figured out a place, in a golden wheat field, behind a wire fence, on the east side of the teacher's outdoor toilet, and off school grounds. Each afternoon during recess, it was decided which girl(s) would be the lookout, to watch for teachers, and keep out boys. The girls paired up and decided which one would pretend to be the boy. Beulah was uncomfortable and did not want to participate, but was afraid to be different, because teachers might ask "what was going on", if she stayed alone at the building. The biggest ordeal, each day was choosing partners, and assigning a lookout to watch for teachers and boys.

Usually activity during recess was walking in pairs or groups, arm in arm, or hand in hand, or arms around each other's waist. Second usual activity, during recess was sitting on the side of the steps and talking. During that era, brick schools were built with broad Granit, cement steps. Built upon each side was as-a-bench.

Uncle Lonnie Woodall was married four times, but only had one son, by his second wife. He and his first wife did adopt a four year old girl, during his first marriage. The girl had real mental problems, because her step-mother use to lock her in the closet. The girl went to a "Girl's Home," during her teen years. She used to tell the cousins about spending time in "solitaire", and cutting her legs with a razor blade.

Frank and Cassie raised their children to believe that "the man was boss". He owned the wife and children and children were meant to be seen and not heard. They were to say "Yes ma'am" and "no ma'am", "yes sir and no sir" to adults. Even to those who were older, and who were in authority. People back then believed if there was an illegitimate child born, in the household, it was considered his responsibility and bore the man's last name.

Family members told about when Cassie was a toddler, she was playing around the big, black, hot vat/wash pot, where her parents were making Sugar Cane Syrup. She fell over into the pot and burned the fingers on both hands. As they healed, her fingers were partially webbed, similar to duck's feet.

It was Beulah's duty to write a letter, dictated by Cassie, to grandma, Ruth about every two months. Cassie only went to the sixth grade. Therefore, she was not very good at reading or writing. She depended on Beulah to fill out and place mail orders to Sears, from the big Catalog, for clothes, for the family, and materials to make dresses, pajamas, etc., as well as household supplies.

It was her sneaky, cowardice way, to have Beulah confront Frank about how he treated her. When she confronted Frank, Cassie would deny all of it. It took Beulah thirty years to figure out how Cassie was using her. Finally she told Cassie, from then on, she could fight her own battles. She did not try that, again. However, her attitude toward Beulah, from that time on, was even colder than before. Beulah, from the time she was a teen, use to say to herself, that Cassie had a yellow streak down her back.

It must have been that Cherokee Indian Heritage in her, Cassie was skilled at doing crafts, making tatting, crocheting, sewing, doing needle work, embroidering, etc. She had a natural talent for fixing things. When the electric iron burned out, or the cord frayed, she would take it apart and repair it. She had a green thumb, we called it. She could snip off a sprig from a bush or tree, stick it in the ground or bucket of dirt and root it. She grew beautiful Dalais, and always had a beautiful yard. She would let other choirs go undone, to haul five gallon buckets of cow manure, for her flower beds, which frustrated Frank.

Cassie looked totally Cherokee Indian. Frank's dad Zech use to make fun of her, intimidate her, and put her down, and call her names, and blaming Frank for marrying her. When truth is known, he had Indian heritage from several different tribes, which he could not hide, because of his coloring. Some people use to call Zech "Nig", he was so dark skinned.

Of the six siblings, the two middle ones (Farris and Saul) were dark skinned like Cassie. The other four were fair skinned, blonde haired, or red headed, Beulah was freckled and reddish, blond headed, Millie and Drusie's hair turned dark as adults. Beulah was the shortest (runt) of the brood. Their youngest brother was bright red headed. Frank had red, curly hair and his friends knew better than to call him "Red". He would never let any of them or anyone else, use nicknames. Grandma Ruth Woodall was red headed.

Sister Millie was born with a bad temper. When she cried, she would get so angry, that she would turn black in the face, and hold her breath. Frank had to slap her to get her to come to her senses. As a toddler, she would get on her all fours, on the floor, cross her legs at the thighs, and masterbate. Frank hated that.

When Beulah was about age 14, Cassie discovered that her wedding ring was missing from the top shelf of the cupboard. She asked Beulah if she had climbed up to see what was in the cabinet, and Beulah admitted that she had, but she did not see her ring. Then Cassie claimed that Albert, the hired hand, could have opened the porch window (near the cabinet) and stolen it. Beulah has always believed that Cassie lost the ring off of her finger, without knowing it, because it would not fit correctly. Due to her webbed fingers she rarely wore it.

Beulah grew up thinking that she had a mental problem,

because her parents treated her differently. She had a heart problem, but every time she had a weak spells or got sick, her parents would say that it was "her nerves". They would not let her go anywhere alone, or do anything strenuous. However, on her seventh birthday, Frank said that she was old enough to go to work. That spring he put a hoe in her hands and taught her how to hoe cotton, and then later pick cotton. She milked cows morning and night, tended chickens, slopped hogs, fed cows, and dog. He had her driving the truck, tractor, and tying sacks on the combine, when she was age twelve. One day he told her he wanted her to drive the tractor over to Egypt, which was acreage he owned a few miles away. He was to follow her in the truck. The roads were not paved, at that time. They were red mud, with deep ruts, from previous rain. One had to drive where the tracks were best. She was sitting upon the tractor, with her blue, striped bonnet on, with him behind in the truck. She glanced back and he was motioning for her to pull over and stop, which she did. He told her that she was "driving on the wrong side of the road".

Once when Drusie and she were tying sacks on the combine, she felt sick, but would never tell her parents. While waiting for the sack to fill up, she laid down in the dump trough. Drusie pulled the cord and dumped her. She fell flat on her back. They had a good laugh, but she could not believe that either one of them would do such a thing. Years later, when she was complaining of back pain Drusie told her that Frank had told her to pull the cord and dump her. Maybe that is when one half of her third Vertebrae was broken off. She had later attributed that to a fall off of the Gater (four wheeler).

Frank thought that she was supposed to learn to do everything on the farm. Cassie thought that she was supposed to learn to do everything, in the house, and had her cooking and sewing at age seven. Beulah use to rip up old family hand-me-down clothes, and remake them for herself, sisters, and Cassie. She made dresses and panties out of flour sacks. They learned how to ravel the threads out of the floral printed sacks and use them for other purposes. They use to say, when a friend would laugh real big "I can see your panties and they are made out of flour sack." Cassie would go to the Cotton field to work and leave the baby with her to attend and leave her to cook "dinner". Dinner was the middle meal of the day, because hands came in from work and need good nourishment to go back to work the rest of the day. It is a conflict, with the family now, when adult children, who have lived away refer to "dinner" as the "supper" meal.

One day grandma Shiloam said to Beulah "you love your grandma Woodall more than you love me". She just turned and gave her a stern look, not knowing what to say. Great grandma Monroe, came out the door with a hand woven trash basket and called to Beulah, as she was leaving down the steps, "Beulah I want you to have this". She was twelve years old. She still cherishes that basket.

Grandma Shiloam was born the night her daddy died with Pneumonia. Therefore, she was able to cure the Thrash during her whole life. When babies in the neighborhood had trash, parents brought them to her. She blew her breath slowly into their mouth while they were screaming and crying, and they were cured. She was the only child. Her dad was red headed. Maybe that is where Frank got his red hair.

Her mama, Macy Monroe was a little Indian woman. She was born from a rape by an Indian man, when her mom was age sixteen. She had long salt and pepper hair, and wore it up in a bun. We could always tell when it was going to rain. The small hairs, on the back of her neck, would curl up. She later married and gave birth to five more children, including a set of twin boys.

CHAPTER TWO

FRANK'S CONTROL

Dt. 20:12 Honor thy father and mother that thy days may be
long upon the land, which thy God giveth thee. KJV

One Sunday afternoon, their family and daddy's siblings and their families were all having a big dinner at Papa Shiloam's. After lunch, as usual, the men went across the road, to Papa's store. The kids went down there. Papa Shiloam filled a small brown paper bag, with Peppermint Candy, from the candy counter, and handed it to the oldest grandchild, and told them to go down in the pasture and pull up "bitter weeds".

Like his mother, Zech had a real bad temper. He despised women. He would call grandma Tallie Shiloam and Cassie "Mammy", and other bad names. He owned farms in South Carolina and Georgia, when Frank was growing up. He owned a Livery Stable and traded horses, in Moose, Georgia. He insisted that Grandma stay at home and refused to allow her to visit sick neighbors. After he died (at age fifty), grandma told about him shooting another young man in the stomach, shortly before they married. It seems that the other man started the fight. Therefore, Papa was never prosecuted. Beulah heard a neighbor say, that He (Papa) was the meanest man who ever lived". She can believe that. Frank told many times of how Papa treated him, but Frank always stood up for Papa. Sounds like Frank was brain washed. Grandma said the reason Frank had problems with his legs, was that Papa made him get into freezing cold water, in the winter time, with his boots on and gather "Sand" for Papa, for Commercial purposes. Frank got angry when Beulah confronted him about that.

Before any of the children had started to school, they and Cassie occasionally spent the night with Grandma Shiloam, while Frank traveled up north to pull down cars. One night they were gathered around the fireplace, and a small Coal sparked out onto Beulah's left little toe. She was so afraid of Papa, that she would not say anything, After a while someone noticed her crying. Grandma got the hot coal off, and put salve onto it.

The children went into the bedroom. Drusie, Aunt Helen, aunt Reba, and Beulah were jumping on the two standard beds. Cassie came in there, went over to get a piece of kindling, to whip them with, but Papa took it out of her hand and bawled her out. He loved to intimidate her.

Beulah and her two oldest sisters started singing as the "Shiloam Trio" before they started to school. They walked across the road to the Presbyterian Church. The superintendent asked them to sing almost every Sunday, and they sang the same song: "Blessed Jesus Hold My Hand", because that was the only song they knew well enough. They continued to minister in Gospel music until 2014, for seventy-six years. The middle sister became ill and had to move to Virginia, with her son. Beulah played the piano and they sang in churches over North Georgia and South Carolina, when invited. They sang on Saturday mornings at the local Radio program, with their pastor's sermons. They had a local Gospel Music Ministry for churches, Senior Citizens, Special events, etc. The Trio sang and played at the Old Time

Singing Conventions in Georgia and South Carolina. They always got an invitation. Usually an offering was taken up, to distribute to the singers for their travel expense. Frank always kept what the girls made. Besides the piano and organ, she played the violin, mandolin, and other string instruments.

Beulah started playing the Piano at age five, and became Pianist at church from age seven until age eighteen, when she married and moved away. Some Sunday mornings her heart Tacky Cardia would kick in and she got nervous before going to church to play the piano, and started crying. Her arms and hands would feel numb. Cassie told Frank. He would come into the kitchen, reach into the top shelf of the Compress Cabinet (Amour), get the bottle of Jack Daniels, pour her about half a jigger, put some sugar or Peppermint candy in it and have her drink it. Those were the times that she went to church and played the piano with whisky on her breath, smelling like Bourbon and thinking nothing of it. They rarely went to the doctor, in those days. If one was sick, they got a home remedy.

Besides the music, Beulah worked in the church as Choir Member, Teacher, Missions Worker, Bible School worker, and did Mission Work for fifteen years.

When Beulah was age seven, Frank and a cousin reopened the small, one roomed Baptist Church, which had been closed for years. She became the pianist, until she married and moved away at age eighteen. They lived just two miles from the church. She played for funerals. When she was a senior in High School, her superintendent called her to his office, handed her his car keys. He told her that his church, out in a community, was holding revival that week and he told her to drive his car to play the piano for them. She refused. Therefore, he went upstairs and brought back a senior boy and told him to drive her there, each of the five days, of the week. Some churches, which she played in, had a pump organ, and she could barely touch the pedals. Some pianos in churches were almost impossible to get a tune out of them. They were so badly in need of tuning. There were no Fans, or Air conditioners, only hand fans. The windows were opened on hot days, and sometimes the wind blew the music off the piano/organ while playing it. The hand fans were donated from Politicians, who had their ads on them. The church was unpainted wood inside and out. The benches were hand made of wood, and there were wooden benches in the Choir. Beulah played the piano and organ under the huge Arbor, during revivals. The Arbor was made with large hewn tree post, and the benches were split, large trees. There was saw dust on the floor/ground. A "Dinner on the Ground" was held the last Sunday of the Revival.

By the time they started to school, (although Drusie was sixteen months younger than Beulah), she was taller heavier, and prettier than Beulah. Frank started them to school together. They went all the way through the twelfth grade together. Cassie dressed them alike and people thought they were twins. Most people thought Drusie was the oldest. Beulah was use to her aunts and uncles doting over her. However, after moving to Georgia, no one every doated over her, or even showed her any affection. When she first started to school, she would not say "finger". She said "Thinger". Her family tried to get her to say it right, but she was stubborn. At school older children started teasing her, and laughing about it. She soon figured out it was "finger".

When she was living with her grandparents in South Caroline, several times when Frank visited, before time for school to start, he raved about she was not going to school there in the city, because" those big ole boys would hurt her". That was all she could imagine "the big ole boys would hurt her", if she went to school anywhere. In 1939, Beulah was age six and a half. Frank tried to start her to school. She refused to go. They put her, Drusie and two aunts on the bus, but Beulah screamed and cried for about two miles, and the driver came back and let her get off the bus.

Frank held Beulah back one year and started Drusie to school one year younger (at age 5) which caused a terrible raucous. The principle (Granny Rooter) must have been in her eighties, and wore her hair up in a bun. No one liked her, or her "Old Maid" daughter who also taught in grammar school.

Granny Rooter was determined to have her way. One solution they came up with was to divide the youngest first graders and the older ones, making two first grades, which required another teacher for the school pay. Beulah and Drusie were each their teacher's pets. Granny Rooter did everything she could to upset Frank. When the girls were in the seventh grade, she was their history teacher. Come report card time, she marked both girls an "F" on history. They both went home crying. Frank went to the school and got that taken care of. Beulah made all "A's" all way through Post Graduate School. Drusie made "B's and C's" and never failed any subjects.

Frank had a brother who was in jail, once, for a speeding ticket. He was very strong willed. In 1940 Papa Zech Shiloam died at age fifty, with Cirrhosis of the Liver. Beulah was only seven years old.

At age nine, Helen and Beulah ran away. Helen got mad at Grandma Shiloam, tied up some clothes on the end of a stick, threw the stick over her shoulder. She came walking down and asked Beulah if she wanted to run away with her. So, they walked down the road, to the end of the property line, then down the line, and sat down in the field on a terrace. Grandma and Granny Monroe came down to Cassie's, and they watched them. They got tired of sitting and went to the house. No one mentioned what they had done.

∞

It came a heavy shower in April, when Beulah was in the third grade. She wore a sailor dress, which someone had given to her. At recess she and the girls ran down back of the school building, to the outdoor toilet. She had to wait for one of the stools to become available. It came a sudden pour down of rain as she ran back to class. Other girls beat her back to the room. She got totally drenched. The teacher spanked her, made the boys start a fire in the large heater, and made her stand in front of it until she became dry. It was one of those huge, round metal casings outside, with a small wood heater inside. There was barely enough wood to start the fire. The teacher had to use a lot of paper to get it started.

In the fourth grade, they danced around the May Pole, in front of the school yard. Each of them had a blue streamer, which ran from the top of the pole. They danced to music while they wove the streamers. Then they danced back, while they unbraided the streamers.

On several summers, their cousin Linda spent the night with them. She slept in the same, bed between Drusie and Beulah. Linda would masterbate while they lay there talking and giggling. She would say "wait a minute" while she reached an orgasm. Beulah figured out later what she was doing. They did not speak about it.

One summer, when she was about eleven years old, a Baptist Church across the river, upon a steep hill, held a revival at night, and needed a pianist. She rode the Ferry over there, with church members. Heth was the one operating the Ferry. That was long before they became sweethearts. However, he did live in the neighborhood, and went to the same school as she.

They washed clothes by starting a fire outside, in the Ole, Black, iron wash pot, heating water, and boiling their clothes, and stirring them. They lifted the clothes out of the hot water with a paddle, and stirred them in clear rinse water, in a galvanized tub.

While the family visited their maternal grandparents in South Carolina, the cow ate Butter Bean hulls, which someone had thrown over the fence, that morning. They found her swollen and dead, when they returned. Of Course, Frank blamed Cassie and the rest of the day was ruined. Every time they visited her family, Frank would always come home and start one of his Shiloam fits, as soon as the car was stopped in the yard. Once they visited her family on a Holiday. When they returned home, while riding in the car, or as soon as they were in the house, Frank pitched a fit, about something he did not like, regarding her family, or what someone said or did. Grandma sat up on the high back steps, with her short dress, her legs sprattled and no panties on, he said. Or, two brother-in-laws did not like what he said about how they should manage their accounts. They were having financial problems.

Beulah was so frustrated; at times she felt she just had to move furniture. WhenFrank came home, he would fuss, saying that he could not find the dresser to comb his hair. He blamed Cassie, as usual.

She use to worry that her parents would die and wondered how she would take care of her siblings. Cassie was so afraid to stay alone with just the children, when Frank would go up north to Chicago, and other places to pull down cars for sale. He would stay gone for one or two weeks at a time. Beulah would always be the first one to greet him, when he returned.

She watched for his car coming around the road, and always hugged him, crying.

Frank would sit down at the table, to eat and push dishes away, occasionally, with his fingers (inch by inch), and snort, like he was about to attack one of them – usually Cassie or Beulah.

She was afraid of her parents and obeyed exactly everything they said. She would not argue or talk back, if she disagreed with them. She would just cry. They would then say she was nervous. She was not allowed to get angry or fuss. She cried when she got mad, and was afraid to speak. Beulah's parents were Authoritarian. They were controlling, demanding, verbally, mentally, and physically abusive to her. She learned early to do exactly what they said, jumping to it quickly. She learned to obey them; therefore it was easy for her to obey God. Beulah use to tell her parents "good night" repeatedly every night, because she could not get to sleep. She was so insecure. They would just get angry and fuss at her. Drusie would hold her hand so she could go to sleep.

Cassie was cruel and fussed at Beulah all day, every day. She followed her around with a switch in her hand and switched her legs, as Beulah worked. Every night Beulah could not go to sleep. She would apologize to Cassie every night, for being so bad. However, she did not know what it was that she did wrong. She had not done anything wrong. She switched on the oldest brother all day the same way. One time he was about two years old. He had a tractor made from an empty spool of thread, with a match stick and a rubber band. He was driving his tractor on the rocks where water poured off the corner of the porch. He was talking about crossing the dam. She spanked him for saying "dam" Drusie told her that he was talking about crossing the dam. She would not apologize.

Growing up, Frank would not let Beulah eat sweets, except

the deserts, on special occasions with relatives. However, on a few occasions, in the late afternoon, after she finished her outside work, there were several times, that she slipped into the kitchen, mixed up one teaspoon each of sugar and cocoa. She then made a paste of the two with milk, and ate all of it, while everyone else was out of the house.

The only toy Beulah ever had was a doll, which Santa brought to her under the Christmas tree, at age ten. She named the doll "Molly". Drusie got one just like it and she named her's "Dolly. That same year Santa brought the two of them a "King James Bible". Several Christmas's after that, Santa brought a new dress for each doll. Beulah discovered that Cassie made them, sewing a little at night. She found them in the clothes press. All six children only got oranges, apples, and a small bag of Pepperment candy, which Cassie put up on the top shelf, of the kitchen cabinet, where they could not reach it. It was saved to help with colds or used in whiskey, for medicine.

One summer morning in June, Frank told Beulah and Drusie to throw the freshly chopped firewood into the woodshed. After a while Beulah threw a stick, while Drusie was moving to throw. It knocked a hole in her head, about four inches above the nose, in her hair line. Blood spewed and both were screaming, running into the house. Cassie fixed a bandage on it.

Another day, Hellen, cousin Corry, and Beulah sneaked down in the cotton patch, picked some white Rabbit Tobacco and chewed it. She got real sick and threw up. On one occasion aunt Helen and grandma Tallie let Beulah dip snuff. Frank found out about it and later gave her a spanking, when she came home. However, it did not stop her from dipping, whenever they would share with her.

Nash Williams (Frank's first cousin) use to say "Beulah is

the only child that Frank has, because he talks about her all the time."

One Sunday afternoon, Drusie and Beulah, and two neighbor girls were allowed by their parents to walk, from the house, a little ways down the dirt road. Beulah made the remark that they were "free" and could go anywhere. Someone must have heard her. When she got home, Frank had her know that he knew everything she said. And always knew where she was. She knew that, because he always made sure that he, Cassie, or Drusie one was always with her., everywhere she went. She would not even hardly go next door, to spend the night with her grandma Shiloam (very few times).

Beulah really loved her fourth grade teacher, Mrs. Colby. At Christmas, she wrapped a "Bobby Pen" and rewrapped it over and over many times, until it was a large package. When the class opened presents, everyone was anxious to see what the teacher got. She became very embarrassed and Beulah felt guilty, when she finally reached the "Bobby Pen".

Cassie decided that Drusie and Beulah should take turns washing dishes, before the school bus came, each week day. One morning when they got on the bus, everyone was laughing at us. Drusie forgot to take off her apron, and got on the bus with it on.

Beulah was baptized at age twelve, in the new cemented Baptismal, in back of the Church Arbor. It was around that time, that she began to have desires to be a Missionary. She mentioned it to her parents several times, while growing up. They would not hear of it. Drusie was baptized at the same time, both in their white outfits.

∞

Beulah and her mama were washing clothes in the old wringer washing machine, on the back porch. She showed her blood stained panties to Cassie, to tell her that she had gotten her first period, at age 12. Cassie immediately began fussing at her, and got stern. Cassie told her to tell her sisters, that Frank said "if one of them got pregnant, he would kill Cassie". She did not tell them.

Cassie had not talked to Beulah, or her sisters about sex, or Ministration. What they knew, they heard from their friends at school, church, or cousins. She thought that her period was supposed to come every thirty days. Therefore, she marked the calendar each month for the same day, as last month's period.

Several times she got her period while at school. Thus, she knocked on the principle's wife's door, which was near the school, and told her that she got her period. The lady was gracious enough that she brought a Kotex and sanitary belt for her. She went back to the school restroom, and put them on. She had not heard of those things before. She figured out later that her mama used rags, from the rag sac, pinned into her panties. After a few times of that happening the lady told her to get her parents to buy her those supplies. From then on, Cassie had Frank buy sanitary supplies for the girls.

At age thirteen, the class was taking a History test. She got out of her seat to take her paper to the teachers desk, when she finished the test. Arriving back at her seat, a friend told her that she had blood on the back of her skirt (about the size of her fist). The teacher had to leave the class, and walk Beulah to the lunch room, where she washed the spot out of her skirt.

When Beulah was in the ninth grade, in 1946, the Principle (who was also her Math teacher) had assigned the class to work the problems in back of the book which only gave the answers. Next day he would try to work them on the board, and asked them to help him work them as he worked. She was the only one who got all the answers correct. No one in the class could work the problems, and neither could he. So, he asked her to come to the board and work the problems, for the class.

∞

Children on the school bus, was making fun of her, Drusie, and their aunt Mary, in 1946. For several mornings, they were telling others not to associate with the girls (their parents had told them). They were crying by the time they unloaded the bus at school, and did not know why they were told this. The teacher made them all come in, sit down, and tell her what was going on. They learned that it was because their grand father (Frank's father, and Mary's dad) was illegitimate, as were all eight of his siblings. His real dad was Spike Turk, a prominant neighbor. Frank's best friend and a church deacon were first cousins, as were their two sons second cousins. Their great grandmother had eight children, and was not married. Their mother (Cassie) was one-forth Cherokee Indian.

Up until that time they had been told by their parents that they were half Iris and half Scottish. They were now told that they were mostly Indian. Cassie was Cherokee and Frank was a mixture of several tribes. Grandpa Woodall's mother was full blooded Cherokee Indian, and looked every bit of it. Beulah's middle sister Farris and brother Saul were dark skin and had black hair, like Indians. Todd her youngest sibling and Beulah were red headed and freckled, like Frank and their grandmother Woodall. The other two girls were blondes.

Drusie and Beulah both bought adult purses, with shoulder straps, just alike, when they were in the eighth grade. They purchased them with money, which they earned from picking cotton. Bessie frequently dressed them like twins. In about the fifth grade Beulah ordered from Sears Catalog material and made them "Wine "colored jumpsuits alike.

In the eighth grade they bought black, high heel sandals, and wore them with their Blue Jeans to school. It took a lot of convincing, but they finally persuaded their dad, that they (like all of the girls Basketball team) needed to start wearing jeans, to play ball in. Back then, girls did not wear slacks or jeans.

When those black "Slides" came out, aunt Reba and Hellen each bought a pair. That was the first Beulah and her siblings had heard of "Sandals". Their parents would not buy them any. So, Beulah went to the wood pile picked out two pieces of wood, for the soles. Then, she went to the rag sack and found two suitable pieces of rags, to tack to the wooden soles. She hobbled around the yard for days in those things.

Ricky Black was a ninth grader, who lived across the road from the school. He would drive his "A" Model Ford to the back of the school and work on it, at recess. While the fourth grade girls, were walking around the school building, holding hands in a line, he would touch the electric current under the hood, of the car, and they could each feel the electrical current down the line.

∞

Grandma Tallie Shiloam's house had a wraparound porch. ("L" shaped). It was an antebellum house, built in 1898, and had a cellar under the back of the house. The family use to sit on the front porch during the daytime looking northwest and see the beautiful Smokey Mountain range. Then at night, they sat on the front porch, looking northeast and could see lights from Sartain, SC airport flashing, and watched planes overhead to and fro. The grandparents would tell tales of ghost, or someone riding bicycles around the porch at night, and of ghost. There was a grave yard joining the east side of the property.

Frank use to brag about riding bare back on his horse, Essie, a sweet, little, black, freckle faced neighbor, wearing a little, black hat, pulled down over the left forehead, lived down below the five forks. She use to walk up to Papa Zech Shiloam's store, just past their house, about once a month. She walked with a stick and when the children saw her coming. They would run out and beg her to tell their fortunes. They would hold out a hand, and she would say "no I don't want that hand. I want the other hand". Then, they would talk her into coming into the house and playing the piano two songs: "Oh, I Want to See Him", and "Looking This Way, Lord". She sang with her mouth full of snuff.

The children made play houses. They played that they were Movie Stars. Aunt Helen was inclined to play as Rita Hayworth. Cousin Corry, usually played as Roy Rogers, Clark Gable, or Gene Autry. Beulah played as other less famous Movie Stars. Usually it was just those three. Sometimes, Drusie and Jewel played with them, but they often had other agendas. Helen played holding her doll after she was twelve years old. People talked about how she would have her own babies, someday. However, that was a different story. She was very in love, as a teen, with a fine hard working country boy, who was a neighbor boy. However, Grandma Tallie, and Frank, would not let her have anything to do with him. She soon met a rich, city boy, which they approved of. They were married, and she soon got pregnant. She would beat her stomach and say "I do not want this baby". Never the less, she named her Precious". She only had one child. She was cruel to her every day of her life. She was horrible to her two grand children (a boy and a girl). She was very jealous of the attention that her husband showed her daughter, rather her to care for him, before he died.

Papa Zech bought two black men, off the County Chain gang, to help work the farm. They lived out in the Smoke House, and slept up stairs. They ate down stairs where the Hams hang.

One was very kind. He use to take the children on rides in the one horse wagon. The other was mean. One kept begging uncle "Rusty" to buy him a bicycle. Finally after a while Rusty bought him a bike. A few nights later he rode that bike over to great grandma Shiloam's house, broke in the window and raped her. Later, the County hanged him.

Frank was frequently fussing about those "sorry Hammonds", his first cousins. They drank alcohol beverages, most of the time, cursed, and would not hardly work, at all. However, Frank loved to carry a bottle of booze over to their house on Saturday nights and get them drunk enough to beat them playing poker. He got out his pocket knife, showed Beulah how he split the right corner of a high card, or scrapped off the ink on the corner of a card, and they did not know the difference.

Frank used to go occasionally with his bible in hand, to visit another neighbor who was an alcoholic with six kids, and a poor overworked wife. Cassie use to stay up at night waiting for him, rocking and crying. She would try to make Beulah go to sleep, but she just lay in bed crying, also, until he returned at a late hour.

One late night, as he walked from the carport to the house, he fell over two benches in the back yard and badly skinned up both legs on the shin. He accused Cassie of placing those benches in his path purposely, so that he would get hurt. Beulah never ever saw the two benches placed in that place of the back yard, before. She could only assume that he supposed correctly. It took a long time for the gashes on his shins to heal. The benches were wooden, about six feet long and ten inches high. He had built them. He placed them on the back porch, a year or so earlier.

Turns out that Beulah figured out from putting some things together, that Harold Gatlin must have been Frank's half brother. Frank told Millie before he died, that his dad Zech pointed out a man crossing the road from the store was Frank's half brother. Papa Zech laughed when he told it. Frank was very hurt and Millie would not reveal the name of the man. However, before Frank died Harold's youngest son was killed in a car wreck and Frank was extremely upset. He would not go anywhere, hardly, not even in his wheel chair, because his spine burned when h e set up straight. He was bed ridden for fifteen years, before he died. However, he insisted on going to that boy's funeral and when he returned he cried uncontrollably. That boy surely looked a lot like Beulah's baby brother. Harold was the spitting image of one of Zech's grandsons.

Beulah was required to pick more cotton than anyone in the field, even the adult hired hands, when she was barely a teen. She was threatened by Frank that, If she did not weigh up at 100 pounds, each day. She would get a spanking. More is required of the oldest child. Unfair.

Frank got so angry, because Todd was so slow to get started harrowing the field. He got the tractor and began to make the rounds, himself. Beulah watched him, as he slung the corner of the field, in front of Todd's house, that the harrow flipped up sideways, each time he came around.

CHAPTER THREE

FIRST KISS

I John. 4:18 there is no fear in love: but, perfect love
casteth out fear, because fear hath torment. KJV

Heth joined the Presbyterian church, and was sprinkled, across the road from her house, as a teen. She was there, and watched it. He was always Pig Headed, and negative about everything. He had to argue all the time over things. Noting was good enough for him. So sad. No joy.

Occasionally, a school classmate invited them to go home with her, to spend the night. Later she would come to spend the night with them. On one such occasion, they both begged Frank to let them go spend the night with her. He was hesitant about giving them an answer. However, with their insistence he finally said Drusie can go. Beulah stay home and milk both her and Drusie's cows, bring in the firewood, and feed the chickens, night and morning, which also meant that she would wash Drusie's share of the supper and breakfast dishes. How unfair!

At age sixteen, Frank carried Beulah and Drusie somewhere in the truck. When they got in, he insisted that Beulah ride in the center. When he changed gears, he ran his hand up and down her legs, turned to her and grinned real big. She frowned at him.

He use to take them to the movies, in town, on Monday nights. Frank had a double standard for life. One for him and a different one for everyone else.

Beulah climbed up (in a chair) to the top Mantle over the fire place, and stole two of Frank's Winston Cigarettes, from the pack. She carried them and some matches to school. She and Debbie smoked them behind the old outhouse at recess. Frank must have learned of it, because he quit smoking shortly after that.

Cassie occasionally had a big pot of Hominy cooking on the small, Franklin heater, when the children came in from school. Beulah could hardly wait to get her a cup full of it.

Grandpa D.J. Woodall died in 1947, at age sixty-five.

∞

Frank was one of the chaperones, on the school bus, from a basketball game, at another school one night. Dennis, a husky, robust, muscled, classmate sat on one side of Beulah and Frank sat on the other side. With no warning and quite unexpectedly the boy grabbed Beulah and planted a sustaining, juicy kiss on her lips. That came out of the blue. Dennis had never made any actions or words in the past to indicate that he was interested in Beulah. She had never even thought about liking him. He had black curly hair, and was very good looking. She had, in the past commented that she would like a boy friend with black curly hair.

His dad died with Muscular Sclerosis. Dennis and his older brother were hard workers. They had to make a living for their mother, sister, and smaller, half brother and sister. Their mother had remarried after their father died. Therefore, he and his brother had to work a crop and could not attend school regularly. They had missed several grades, because of poor attendance.

It was a cold winter night; she and Drusie were getting ready for Frank, to take them, to the school house, to play basketball. She was ready to go and standing around waiting on Drusie to get ready. Frank looked at her, and said to Beulah "I know what you are thinking about, that boy". Dennis's uncle had told Frank that Dennis had the same disease that his dad had, and would not live long. Beulah did not know that, until several years later.

Drusie and Beulah had worked hard picking Cotton. Frank took them to town on Saturday and let each buy a wrist watch, with their hard earned money. Soon after, Dennis politely took Beulah's watch off of her arm (forcefully), put it on his arm (really stretching it), wore it home and she did not see it for months Frank asked her about what happened to her watch, months later. She told him. He told her to tell him to bring it back to her. She told Dennis what Frank had said. He soon brought the watch back. He had taken the back off, had it all apart (his brother said), and it looked very used.

Dennis soon started coming to Beulah at recess, escorting her to the Principal's office and let her pick out what candy she wanted, and he bought it for her. The second grade teacher made Peanut Butter Fudge and other candies and sold them in the office, five days a week. Frank had never wanted Beulah to eat sweets, and pitched a fit, at the table, every time she touched a desert. God only knows why. She felt so pampered and very much enjoyed the candies.

First recess, one morning coming from the candy treat, coming out the door of the office, the stairs was just right of the door. Dennis grabbed her right arm to go upstairs. SHE WAS AFRAID/SCARED!. She resisted all she could saying "no". He drug her anyway, up to the auditorium and back to a room behind the stage. He kissed her on the mouth repeatedly. Drug her by the wrist over to the window, raised the window and yelled out to the friends on the ball field. She broke to run. She had on the 2" heeled, black sandals, which she had bought with her cotton money, and she had on jeans. The principle heard her running, and came up there. He made them both get back down stairs, and sent Dennis home.

Dennis started coming to church and sitting beside Beulah on the front row, where she played the Piano. One week they were having revival, under the large, old Arbor made from huge, hewn trees. He came every morning and night. Frank became furious. Years later, at a church function, Dennis' brother told her and friends, how much Dennis was in love with her, while sitting at the table with her husband and other school mates. He told about how far Dennis walked across fields to church just to be with her.

Soon after Dennis asked Beulah to marry him. She said "no". She did not even know whether she liked him or not. She certainly liked the attention, but she had never planned to get married.

Dennis and Rush were both on the basketball team, and Rush was Drusie's boyfriend. He and she use to take Beulah to the movies with them at night. Frank had said that neither of them could date, but she did anyway, and Frank acted as if he did not notice. Rush's dad was the song leader at church, and a neighbor. So Frank trusted them. One night Rush brought a box of Chocolate covered Cherry candy, handed it to Beulah and said that Dennis sent them to her, and said that he loved her. She carried them into the house, under her coat, hid them in the bottom, back of the Shift robe, and sneaked one out after school, until they were gone.

Heth had written his cousin Rush that he was planning to ask Beulah to marry him, when he came home from boot camp.

Rush told his dad who ran a barber shop, and it was all over town before she knew it.

The day before he came home from Navy boot camp leave, Dennis called her at the Insurance office where she was secretary, and said "I heard that you are going to get married". She just hung up and never heard from him, again.

Dennis later married one of Beulah's Cheerleader partners. She was dark headed, small, and had a Bubbly personality, very much like Beulah. They built a large, beautiful, brick house in town. She became a nurse, and he became deathly sick. He only lived a few years after they were married. Beulah saw his son once, after he was grown, at church with his mother. He was the very image of his dad. The boy got hooked on drugs, and died at an early age. His mother died soon after with cancer. The house sat empty for years, before it finally sold.

Drusie was very jealous of Rush. One day as class was returning to the room, from recess, he grabbed Beulah, outside the door, planted a huge wet kiss smack on her mouth, not to her liking, and much to her surprise. He must have gone directly and told Drusie, claiming it was consenting. When they returned home that afternoon, she threatened her in no uncertain terms, that she was to stay away from Rush. He became her husband a few years later. Beulah had never been attracted to him. He was a spoiled, overgrown baby, the only boy and youngest of two sisters. He smoked since a very small child. He die at age sixty-eight, with lung cancer. He used to arbitrarily date Drusie's best friend, occasionally, just to make her jealous, or maybe it was for what he got.

∞

In Economics class they lacked enough pans, and the teacher asked her to put her biscuits on the baking sheet with another girl. Beulah won the baking contest and the other girl tried to claim that the biscuits that won were her's. She was the sister to Dennis. Later, while getting out of class at recess, one morning, the same girl (the largest girl in the class, who was a bully) grabbed her, telling her to wait. When everyone else was gone out of the room, she backed Beulah in a corner, and started beating her in the stomach with her fist. Beulah could not say or do a thing, but take it. . She figured that it was to get her back, because she won the Biscuit Contest. After Dennis became enamored with Beulah, the girl became her best friend and protected her from others.

When Beulah and Drusie were in their early teens, Frank made them go with him to sit over night with corpses, in people's homes. Back then, bodies lay in people's living rooms after they were embalmed, until the funeral. People were visiting all hours of the day and night to look at the body, and to honor the family.

The only time Beulah can remember Cassie showing affections to her, was when she was in her late teens. She was dressed up to go play the piano, for church service. Cassie came up to her, smiled and said that she just wanted to hug her, because she looked so beautiful. Otherwise, she never showed Beulah any affection. She just carried that Peach tree twig and switched her legs and arms, saying "hurry up and get it done."

From age seven until age eighteen, Beulah had "Boils" on her bottom, frequently. She never told anyone until she married. Then she told her husband. After she married and moved away, she did not have them anymore. In her seventies, while at the dermatologist, when the doctor was out of the room, she told the nurse about it, and that they had started again since moving back to Georgia. The nurse told her that it was a "Staff Infection", and that they can lie dormant until some illness triggers it. She said they do not respond to medications, except antibiotics. Beulah must have had antibiotics for another illness which got rid of them.

While Beulah was a senior in high school, she became sick. Her parents carried her to the doctor and had her tested to see if she had sex or was pregnant. She was a virgin. They did not tell her what they were doing, but when the nurse put her in stirrups, then came back and told her to get up, she figured it out.

The only time a principle every came to their door about anything or anyone, he came to inform Beulah that she had been nominated to be "Miss Twin Oak School contestant, to represent the 4-H Club. She had her dad to drive her to town, bought some blue Chiffon material and some blue net material and made her dress for the event. She made a fitted waist with short sleeves, a gathered skirt, and the net covered the full Chiffon skirt.

During her senior year in high school, Beulah was in the Drama class. She was in the Play "All on account of little Nell." She won the first place Drama, blue ribbon at the State Try Outs. She was in two Beauty Contest, was a Cheerleader, in the Beta Club, School Choir, School Trio, Pianist at home church, played for all community funerals, and each parent kept her busy all the time when she was at home. She got sick and the Medical Doctor diagnosed her as being fatigued, put her to bed for a week (at home) and on medication to make her sleep most of the time. After a few days, Frank made her get up and go to work around the farm.

Heth quit school in the seventh grade. His dad made him work a crop. He was glad to go back to school, in the seventh grade, the next year. His dad was a bootlegger. The sheriff was frequently after him. He made Heth hide whisky bottles under pasture post. When Heth was age fifteen, He tried to kill his older brother Daren. They were going out to the barn to hook up the plows and go to work. He tried to hit Daren over the head, with the plow stock, but his mom saw what was going on and stopped him. Years later Beulah asked Heth why he wanted to kill Daren. He said that Daren had a job sweeping floors in the Cotton Mill, and bought a new coat. Heth was jealous because he did not have a new coat like Daren's.

Heth was a football player, in High School, and Beulah was a Cheerleader. Students graduated at the end of the eleventh grade, until 1950 when the twelfth grade was added. Heth got to go another year to play ball. He and Beulah went to the Senior Prom together that year.

Beulah wanted to go to College, after she graduated. She was an honor student with a 4.0 record, and she wanted to be a Missionary. She could have applied for a grant easily. However, her dad would not let her go. He told her that somebody had to stay there and help make a living for all the family. She cried for six weeks. God was so good to give her the opportunity to go to College, after she married. Praise is to God.

∞

The county school she attended only went through the ninth grade. Therefore the tenth through the eleventh and later twelfths were bused to town. When she started to High School, the Home Economics teacher called her in and told her not to sign up for Home Economics, because there was nothing else they could teach her. She told her that she could come in sometimes and help her teach. She graduated from High School in 1951. Her History teacher liked to hear her laugh, and nicknamed her "Sunshine".

Beulah worked, as secretary for an Insurance Agency, after school hours. She made $20.00 a week. Mostly just sitting there and answering the phone, which rarely ever rang? She rode on the bus, to school mornings, and home in the evenings, with a neighbor who worked in town. He did not charge anything for the ride, because he had to come by their house on his way to work. She was already trying to figure out how she could move out, knowing that her dad would not allow it.

One summer Beulah and Dennis (age 17 months) spent a week with grandma Woodall. One night Beulah asked her why doctors said that she would not live when she was born. She said that Beulah had a heart problem and a long, difficult birth. Therefore, her head was shaped like a cone. She said that when she bathed her, she would always pray and rub her head. It took about a year for her head to grow normal. Sturgeon love, is the love that gravitates to a person, or thing, etc.

One Sunday while driving home to Marlo, NC, she was crying about having to leave her parents, and siblings. Heth reached over, while he was driving, and slapped her across the face. She just cried even harder.

The family took baths on Saturday nights. Drusie and Beulah made a fire in the fireplace which was in their bedroom, filled a wash pan with water, each got a wash rage and they used the same bar of soap, to take a "Sponge Bath". In the summertime they all went barefooted and had to wash their feet in a wash pan of water, at night. Aunt Reba Shiloam use to laugh and tell how Beulah hated to wash her feet, and she still does.

Cassie did not wear make-up, because Frank would not let her. She use to before she married him. It was a regular Sunday morning fuss, about 9:45am when she tried to sneak out the door with very light lip stick on. He told her that he would not leave, until she removed it. He told her what she could and could not do about everything. She would not go shopping or leave home, except to visit her family and go to church. She did not wear slacks, because the men in church forbid their wives to wear them. Frank was very controlling. Neighbors and relatives talked about Beulah was the only child Frank had, because she was all that he talked about. She resented them saying that. He alienated two of his brother-in-laws, Cassie's brother-in-laws, while talking about how to handle their finances. He put them down for not knowing how to manage their money.

Cassie did not clean house. Therefore, Beulah took the initiative to sweep and dust. One day Cassie told her "I am never coming to see you, when you get married, because you won't keep your house clean." Go figure? There was red Georgia dust on everything, from where they were tar and graveling the road, trash on the floor, and cob webs in every corner, etc. They had all windows up, because they had no fans. She would browbeat her. Cassie was very jealous of Beulah. Her parents did not visit her but three times after she married. They never gave her anything. No wedding gifts, and no baby gifts. Heth's mother gave them a beautiful pair of pink pillowcases with lace trim. Although they were second hand, because someone had given them to her. Beulah cherished them, and knew that they were the best that she had.

One hot Saturday, August evening, the family, including the in-laws and grandchildren, were making Ice Cream in a hand cranked churn, on the back porch, at Frank and Cassie's house. Frank sat down with all his weight and force, on a folding chair, on the porch. It broke, and his head hit the outside wall of the house. It made a large "goose egg" on the back, center of his head. He threw a Shiloam fit (what they called his temper tantrums), blaming Cassie for putting the chair there. He said that he told her not to put that chair there. She did not respond. They all knew that was not true. He was blaming the accident on her.

Another evening, in the heat of summer, Frank unharnessed the one mule and one horse, and let them run around in the lot, in front of the barn. After a little while he tried to round them up to go into their stables. The Mule would not go into the stable. He just wanted to romp around and play. Frank got tired and angry fooling with him. He picked up the Pitch Fork and threw it at the Mule. It struck him in the side near his back hip and the horse wobbled into his stall. He almost died. Frank was ashamed to get a Vet to come out. He just put Watkins Salve on the wound, daily for weeks. The whole family watched this take place, and no one ever mentioned it.

∞

Heth came home on a Sunday. They went for a ride that afternoon. He asked "can you get off work, tomorrow"? He never asked her if she would marry him. She did not respond. After a while, she asked "are we going to get married?" He suggested that they go to a near by, large city, next day, and get a blood test, and pick out wedding rings. She agreed. Come to find out after they got there, that an old girl friend still had his metal driver's license, and he needed to go by where she worked to get them, first. They went by, but she went home, at lunch to get them, and she did not return to work. He had worked in that town for a year after finishing High School, in a Tire Shop. He had dated her during that time. That night when he carried her home, she showed the engagement ring to her parents, which he had bought that day, and told them that she was going to get married, the next day. They said "no you are not". She said "yes I am", and that was it.

She got married in 1952. Heth was in the Navy, during the Korean war, doing nine months overseas, and three months in the U. S. She knew that she was marrying beneath her spiritual belief, and financial level, but it was the only way available out of her abusive, dysfunctional home, at the time. He definitely married above his element, but they both were raised on the farm, and at least knew how to make a living. Eros love is Romantic love.

When she got married, she had not learned to make decisions for herself. She had always been told what to do. She did not know how to go to a supper market and shop. Her granddad owned a grocery store and service station. So they usually got their groceries from his store.

Beulah was a virgin when she got married, but her husband was far from a virgin. He loved to boast about his sexual encounters, most of which were with cousins or school friends, which she knew. He would laugh while telling his stories. She thought that was the way all boys did.

When their first son Daniel was born in 1953, Heth was overseas on a heavy cruiser, in the Japanese waters. They got married on his first leave home from Boot Camp, and he only had one week at home. They got married the third day he was home. With four nights left in that week, relatives invited them to spend the nights with them. Each place they stayed they were served "Oyster Stew", and none of the hosts knew that.

One time when they arrived by bus in San Diego, California, near night, they walked, carrying their suitcases, to try finding an apartment. People would not rent to them, because they said she was not more than age thirteen, and not 18. They tried to convince them that she had her marriage license to prove she was eighteen, but they refused to look at them. They finally found an apartment, about dark.

The Navy had decided that Heth should be circumcised. Unexpected by her, this was the beginning of the rejecting her. It could be physical or circumstantial. At the same time, he had made up his mind that he wanted to go to College on the G. I. Bill, and have a career. He sprang this surprise on her by writing that he had "had a surprise for her". When he asked her how she felt about him having a career and going to College, she said that it would be alright with her. He constantly grew more stuck up and hateful to her. Over the years, he repeatedly would say to her "just stick with me and some day you can have everything you want". But, that day never came. He became more selfish, stingy, and conceited. He accused her of seeing Dennis while he was oversea. Dennis never even contacted her. She never saw him during that time, nor thought about him. She did have nightmares about him for about twenty –five years, because of the way Frank treated her and exaggerated the whole relationship. Frank was jealous of Beulah. Agape love is the love that still keeps on loving, when one is not worth loving.

Frank just had to control Beulah's money, when she started getting her government check, after she married. He picked out a nice house in town, owned by a business, lady, friend of his. He told Beulah about it, talked her into buying it, and making monthly payments. He carried her to town to make the purchase. That was his way of trying to keep her living in the same county as him. After Heth got out of the Navy, they sold the house, and moved to South Carolina. She never even went into the house, and they never lived in it. Frank kept it rented out for them. Years later they sold it.

Frank was in the free Masons and Cassie was in the Eastern Star. As soon as Beulah turned eighteen, they had her in the Eastern Star, and as soon as she married, they had Heth in the Free Masons. After they moved away they both demitted, because neither was about Jesus Christ. Phileo love is the love one has for family and friends.

Beulah worked in a sewing plant, while Heth was overseas. Cassie kept Daniel, while she was at work. He was four months old before Heth first saw him, when he came home for Christmas leave.

When Daniel was age nineteen months, they visited grandma Woodall for a week. She told how she chewed up Green Beans and other vegetables, and put them in Beulah's mouth to swallow, to teach her how to eat.

Frank was wild. He loved to tell about riding the bareback horse, down the lane, standing on the horses back, barefooted and no saddle, or anything.

When they would ride somewhere, Frank would point out the farms and say "you can tell who is boss, of that family, by the number of barns". He was so chauvinistic. One afternoon, after Beulah had left home, all four of his barns burned down. They never knew if someone set them afire, or if sparks from another yard trash pile burning blew that way. It really humbled Frank. He was not so Braggadocios' after that.

Frank and Uncle Lonnie drove Beulah, Heth, and Daniel; and another couple from N. C., on their second trip to California. Daniel was a toddler, about nineteen months old. On the road, Beulah threw a wet diaper out the window, and it flew back and hit the window, which startled everyone.

Heth quit the football team, when the coach cursed him. He stayed home from school, until the coach told him that he would not curse him, again. Heth's mom use to tell her about he would come home from school, and disappear. He would go down into the woods and stay until dark. He told her that he was looking for firewood. Beulah asked her if he ever brought wood home. She said no, maybe once or twice.

Cassie had Agoraphobia, and would not go shopping. Once the four girls carried her shopping in the winter time, and she would not buy anything. Only time she had ever been in a mall. So, they all pitched in and bought her a pair of leather, knee boots, to wear to the milk barn, to milk the cows. She never wore them. She would go to the chicken pen, or horse barn, and get Manure to work around her flowers–while Frank fussed. Heth is so much like her, in that way, about gardening. It never ceases to amaze Beulah how much those two are alike, including slow as cream rising on buttermilk. Beulah frequently tells Heth that he will be late for his own funeral. He is usually a day late, and a dollar short. Beulah would watch Cassie nibbling on Graham Crackers, etc. while hanging clothes.

Only one boy ever asked Beulah for a date, in high school. She told him "no" because she was afraid to ask her dad, and she was afraid to be alone with a boy.

Heth's aunt use to cock her head sideways purse out her lips and sullenly say "Heth is going to be a preacher, someday." She loved to keep saying that. Heth never responded. Just because he was so quiet, did not mean that he was so good.

Drusie, Beulah, and Rush went on their senior trip to Washington, DC, part of the way by train, and part by water (Cruise). A friend of Franks had Ice Cream delivered to their room, which was shared by several girls. They were touring when it was delivered. One of their classmates shared it with other girls and it was gone, when they returned. They did not get one bite of it. When they tried to question the guilty girl, she acted a bully. So, they just let it go. When they were in the deli line, Beulah was in front of Drusie and Rush (they were sweethearts). At the checkout counter, Beulah lacked .03 having enough change. Rush paid it for her. She was so embarrassed.

Beulah and Heth had a Gospel Music Ministry starting at her age 16 and his 18, for sixty-four years.

Drusie ran away at age 17 and married Rush. When Frank found out about it, they said he cried like a baby. Aunt Reba told Beulah "Beulah, you were not the one who broke your daddy's heart. It was Drusie." That happened while Beulah and Heth lived in California the first time. Beulah and Drusie married first cousins. Each had two sons. When they were small, they could not understand why they had one Grandma/pa Shiloam, and two grandma/pa Ross. The boys were first cousins and second cousins.

Cassie told both the girls, Drusie and Beulah, to take turns ironing, one Saturday afternoon. It was a large, whole weeks laundry, for the eight family members. Beulah ironed her half, but no matter how much Cassie called Drusie to come iron, she did not respond. Cassie made Beulah do her half of the chores, after she had already done her own half, was very tired and felt mistreated. While she ironed Cassie stood behind her and switched her legs (repeatedly), with a Peach tree switch, saying "Hurry Up", and saying that she was not doing it fast enough. Finally Beulah turned toward her, without saying a word, she reached and grabbed the switch, and looked very stern and angrily at Cassie. Cassie looked very scared and started to cry. She never switched Beulah again, and stopped abusing her.

CHAPTER FOUR

SERVING THE U.S. NAVY

Psalm 15:6 in the house of the righteous is much treasure;
but in the revenues of the wicked is trouble. KJV

rank alienated two of his brother-in-laws, Cassie's
brother-in laws, while talking about how to handle
finances. He put them down for not knowing how to
manage their money. He was very controlling. Neighbors and
relatives talked about Beulah was the only child Frank had,
because she was all that he talked about. She resented them
saying that.

It was a beautiful, peaceful, gorgeous day, while Beulah and
family ate at the lunch table. The country folks eat breakfast,
lunch, and supper, because field hands eat the biggest meal mid
day. Their children live in Mississippi, and Tennessee, and the
parents eat breakfast, lunch and dinner. When in the presence
of them or their friends, the parents try to use the words dinner,
because the word supper creates confusion.

Frank felt the need to tell Beulah what was wrong with her,
when she was born, while at the supper table. He got up to the
point of telling her, then abruptly looked over to Cassie and said

"you tell her". Suddenly, everyone was quiet and nothing more was said.

During one of Heth's leaves, from the Navy, he made a whole roll of films of Beulah, in the nude. After he left, Beulah picked them up from the Drug Store, and not one of them developed. All negatives were solid black.

First time Heth came home from overseas, he told Beulah that, when he boarded the ship the officer asked him "what did you get married for?" He said that he replied "she is working". About a year later, his mom told her, "I told him that you can't marry for money." She just could not see it, then. However, as time/years went on it became very obvious that was exactly what he did.

Heth, on his first leave had asked Beulah if it was alright with her if he went to college after he got out of the Navy, and she said "yes". From that time on, it was like she was his slave. He worshipped "MONEY". Beulah and the two sons had to scrimp and live as if they were paupers. He would promise them "just wait, trust me and someday you can have everything you want". Well, that day never came. He grew more like a "Scrooge" every year.

Second time Heth came home on furlough, Drusie, Rush, and Beulah drove to Atlanta to meet him on the Train. When the train came in he was not to be found, after all the passengers scattered, they were convinced he was not home. Beulah cried all the way home, for two and a half hours. When they arrived home, he was in the bedroom building a fire in the small, iron heater - all smiles, like he was the cutest thing in the world. He told her that Davin Warsh (their preacher's son) had asked him to ride home with him. They had left, before Beulah got there.

Devin was one of the only two known Homosexual guys in that county. Back then people, in that area, just never knew of that kind. They were still in hiding. She asked Heth "did Devin try to come onto you". He said "yes". He said Devin put his hand on his knee. Then, Heth asked him "what is this?" That was all. Of course, she still lives with the pain of that, and more.

Frank and Uncle Lonnie drove Beulah, Heth, Daniel, and another couple from N.C, on their second trip to California. Daniel was a toddler, about eight or nine months old. On the road, Beulah threw a wet diaper out of the window, and it flew back and hit the window, with a big bang, and splash It startled everyone in the car. They already had plans to drive out with his sailor friend and wife from North Carolina. Frank had plans to spend the night with his friends, who lived out there. Beulah cried a lot, would not eat supper, and went to bed crying. She never told anyone what she was crying about. They all ignored her. Frank wanted Cassie to go on the trip, but she declined.

Frank and Heth wrote letters to each other, while he was in service, without Beulah knowing it. Heth thanked Frank for raising such a wonderful wife for him (making points for himself). Frank wrote for Heth to make her mind and behave herself.

Heth had four years of service in the Navy, on the Pacific Ocean. He went out to sea for nine months, (Japan, Korea, etal), His ship came into Dry Dock for three months a year. He came after her and they moved to California for those three months.

They lived in a Quonset hut twice when they lived in California, on Troy Island. The Quonset Huts had two apartments in them, one on each end. Second time they lived in California they shared a Quonset hut. They had the first bedroom across from the living room, Blake and Evy had the bedroom across from the kitchen and bathroom. They were from one of the mid-eastern, southern states and their food desires and some habits were quite different from the Georgia folks. He declared that he would never have any children, but ending up having six, over the years. They played Canasta, all night long on weekends. The two couples divided the cost of groceries. So, Blake decided to move his mother and small brother in with them. They had to sleep on a cot in their back bedroom. Heth and Beulah tried to convince them that they were not liable for half the groceries after his mother and brother moved in. But, they insisted that it stay the same as it had been. UNFAIR! Blake use to tell Heth that he made out with Beulah, while Heth had duty. She could not tolerate him, and Heth knew that. The weather in California was around High 70-80, Low 21-14. Once when they were out there, they barely saw any sunshine. It stayed foggy and misty, most of the time.

While Heth was overseas, and her husband was also, her best high school friend, with their one year babies (hers a boy, and friend's a girl) rented two rooms of the house where she had been raised. They did not have running water or indoor toilet. Her brother-in-law, and his wife, lived in the other two rooms. Their kitchen was a built in back porch with not even room to put an eating table in. There was no sink. Just a small table to hold the water bucket with a dipper, a wash pan, and a bar of soap, with a few cans of food. Frank's Store was in walking distance. So, they did not stock up on groceries. Both of their husbands were in the Korean War. Her's was in the Air Force.

Heth got out of the Navy in July of 1956. That is when he started to college at Calimus SC. There he worked in a Motel after school classes, into the wee hours of the night, as a bellhop, where he also washed their money. He only got paid tips. He had a bachelor friend about twenty-five years older than he was who was a retired professor, who lived alone there. One Christmas Heth came home with seven dollars change, handed it to Beulah, and said (called the man's name) "he said that he saw you and your oldest son eating in the restaurant, at the Motel, and he wanted to give you something for Christmas", WEIRD! To this day, she still wonders if he was easing his conscience, because of his relationship with her husband. Within that year, that man slit his wrist, and committed "suicide". He was later found in his bathtub dead.

She saved pennies to buy him a desk, and also saved change to buy him a Sports Coat. He made her take the Coat back and fussed about spending money for the desk (cheap desk). Sic.

At Christmas he bought her a plastic shoe case to hang over the closet door, for a dollar. That was her Christmas.

Heth and Beulah took ballroom dance lessons at night, at Calimus University. He did not want to, because he was so shy. She convinced him. He loved it, and tried to show out, slinging her around, etc. They won a Ballroom dance contest, given by the city of Raines, MS, in the nineties, and won a twelve piece set of Christmas dishes.

He went to school, on the G.I. Bill. He had to repeat remedial Math and English subjects. He could not do the work. She sat up late hours with him trying to help him comprehend what he was reading. She spent hours on each math problem trying to show him how to work it. He has never told her "thank you" or showed any appreciation, for her help, to this day. He just resents and hates her for being smart. On several occasions during their marriage he has said to her (with all the contempt he could muster) "I know that you are smarter than I am." She has always tried to be patient, understanding, and kind with him, because she always felt so sorry for him. He had such a hard childhood, and was very poor.

Late one night he sat at the desk which she had saved pennies and purchased for him (he resented that). He was pouring over his books, and she asked him to come to bed with her. He hauled off and slapped her real hard across the face, while she was eight months pregnant.

In the 50's, while Heth was overseas, Beulah kept the store for Frank to go buy whole sales. A salesman came by selling furniture polish. She let him leave six bottles for the shelf, with the idea that if they did not sell, he would pick them up later. Frank was so furious, when he returned, that he made her pay him for all of them, and she had to take them and try to sell them to friends. It took a very long time.

Gramdma Woodall died in 1955, at age sixty-five.

They were only living together a few weeks, after they married, when Heth talked her into letting him make love in unusuall ways. He said that his buddy says he and his wife does that. From then on it grew more regular. He did not want to make love often, but that became the habit. It seemed the only way that he could get an erection, most of the time. She had a cluster of tumors removed from her Anus. The doctor said they were almost cancer. After fifty-four years she got tired enough of it. She told him that she did not want to have sex anymore, because it is not worth the effort.

A few days after Heth got back, they were eating Oyster Stew for supper. Heth was holding Daniel on his lap and feeding him. Heth spilled the hot soup on Daniel's foot. You never heard a baby scream so loud. Beulah fussed at Heth for being so careless. He kept saying "I did not mean to". The landlady came over to see what was wrong.

After Heth graduated from Calimus University, in 1959, they moved to Roach, SC. He worked one month for Chelsia Company, and was fired, for doing work himself. The Union Company required him to write up the employee for not doing the work. But, he told Beulah that he was fired because she called him at work one night during a terrible storm and flood. Later she heard him telling his cousin what happened.

While he was out of work for two months, their second son was in the hospital for a week with Asthma and almost died. Beulah stayed with him night and day. It was very hard leaving her five year old son with strange neighbors, for a week.

Heth found a job with Raul's Company, in Mario, NC. They rented a small four room house, which had never been painted, on the railroad tracks. While there they experienced the largest, heaviest snow storm they had ever seen. It was two feet deep, on the car. One church lady told Beulah that her little boys were the cleanest children she had ever seen. Their dad kept their hair cut GI style.

Heth was in the garment industry, after getting out of the Navy, and finishing College. They had two sons, and he was in the garment Industry for forty years, during which time they moved over thirty times. They made the rounds three time from SC, NC, GA, and MS. Beulah and Daniel stayed with her parents in Georgia, when he was over -seas. On three occasions she moved to California, when his ship was in dry dock. One of those times Daniel was with them there.

Third time his ship went into dry dock; he wanted her and Daniel to come out there. Frank got sick with chest pains, and indigestion (Acid Reflux). He was just going to die and did not want them to leave him. She really did not want to go, again. Heth got very upset. They did not learn until many years later that Frank had the same heart problem that Beulah had.

After they moved out of her parents house, and he started College, she taught Daniel (age 4) to stop calling her "Mama", and start calling her "Mother". She could not teach him that before, because Frank put women down.

After a few weeks, Daniel got homesick for Georgia and his

grandparents. So, they packed up his clothes, carried him, on a Sunday afternoon, to her parents, and left him, until he got homesick, for his mother. Then, a week later, they packed up his clothes and brought him home.

Beulah worked in a sewing plant, on a line, stitch stepping, when she got married. She kept up two lines, when a sewer was out sick etc.

She was slightly Claustrophobic, and afraid to ride in elevators.

Heth stayed gone more than half the time. He always had to travel on his work. Beulah practically raised their two sons, alone. She has a Guardian Angel watching over her. The Holy Spirit groans for her, for things she does not even know. She has Jesus who prays for her. Their second son was born (Moses Ross) in Sartain, SC.

Both sons were baptized at the same time, ages 11 & 6.

Frank drew Beulah's picture about 2" x 2" in a small "Blue Horse" notebook, wrote a book about her, and gave it to her. He told her how much he loved her and why he did things the way he did, because he loved her so much. She read it, resented it, and it angered her. She returned it to him and would not comment on it. Her sister Farris, years later, told her that she got the book and took it from Frank's house, to keep him from thinking about it. Years later she claimed that she could not remember what she did with it. She said that she probably burned it.

They were driving with their boys, to Atlanta, to a football game. Heth was angry at her for something she said. They were in heavy traffic, about to get to the stadium on a four lane highway. He speeded up, then slammed on the breaks trying to slam her through the windshield. That was before seat belts were invented.

He told Beulah to get a job. She went to an insurance

company, because she had experience in that work. The man
next door, in the same building, heard her and said "send that
girl over here, she is just what I need". He owned a Credit Bureau
and Collection Agency, and was trying to sell it. She had never
heard of a Credit Bureau. She went home and told Heth. He said
"buy it." So at age twenty-nine, she went to the bank, borrowed
the money and bought it. She made money twice as much as
his salary, and he had been to College, but she had only a High
School Education. People tried to tell her that she would need to
have a Marketing Degree to run it. However, it was a "piece of
cake" for her. He was so jealous, and declared for years that he
would get it one way or another. In 1975 he finally got it. When
she sold the business to move to Mississippi with him, he took
her name off of the joint checking account, and would only
buy groceries. She had to use the money from the sell to pay
house payments, all the insurance, two boy's college tuition, and
anything else that came up. When her money was all spent, and
he wanted her to move with him to North Carolina, he put her
name back on the joint checking account. He moved her again,
WITHOUT HER CONSENT.

One day they visited her parents, Frank told her, "Beulah
don't ever marry a black person". She said "daddy I am already
married". He shrugged his shoulders, jerked his shoulders back,
turned up his nose and said "HUMPH."

Shortly afterwards, Beulah was in the hospital with fatigue
and symptoms of Endometriosis. Heth carried her to the hospital
in Asia, Georgia, one and a half hours away, had her checked into
the Psychiatric Ward, and told them that it was her daddy that
kept her upset. When her parents came to visit her he would
not let her parents see her. That was a blatant lie. Well half a lie.
What she was upset about was that he forced her to go to work,
"to help him have something." His words. Then, he refused to

have sex. He told her that other people have sex "once a year" or "once every six months." He treated her like dirt. He did nothing but went to work, sat at a desk all day, and pushed a pencil. She kept house, washed clothes, hung them at lunch time (they did not have a dryer), drove the boys to school and picked them up after school. She and the boys had to cut the grass and maintain the yard. When he was not at work, he played golf or some kind of sports with his buddies. He spent her money going on vacations and trips when she had to go to Seminars, and out of town meetings. She carried him and the boys with her. She had four employees at the office, covered eight cities, and three counties.

A friend told her "if you are ever going to have an affair, make sure it is with a man who is "Somebody.". She never forgot that. First time he was going out of town on a trip for his company, when they and the boys started to bed, he told them that he was planning to leave in the morning. She and her seven years old cried and begged him all night not to leave, asking why he was planning to leave, and he would not tell them. Finally before time to get up he showed her a $700,00 expense check, which his company had given him for a week's work in Alabama. He said that he was planning to leave and not come back. Their little boy had to go to school that morning without a good night sleep, and she had to go to work. SHAME! SHAME! SHAME! This jerk never apologizes for anything. His dream was to be president of a large industry, someday. She was his ticket to get there.

CHAPTER FIVE

PURSUING RICHES

Psalm 53 my voice shalt thou hear in the morning, O Lord.....I
direct my prayer unto Thee and will look up. KJV

Beulah had to get lost before she could get found. For years Heth use to tell her that if she ever got fat, he would divorce her. He yelled at her to go to work and help him have something. He told her that if she wanted to make love, she could go find someone else and don't let him know about it. Several times he told her that "other people only make love once a year." Later he said on several occasions, "once every six months."

She did Credit Reports nationally and internationally, as well as did reports for Dun and Bradstreet, the Federal Government, and all Military Branches. At that time she had not been to College.

He had a BS Degree and had been employed in the garment industry for five years. Her income doubled what his salary was. People in management at his company told her that she could not run the business, because she needed a Marketing Degree. The job was smooth and easy for her. She loved it.

He bought a fishing boat with the money they made off

the house they sold, before they moved there. They had paid $30,000.00 for the house, lived there six years and then sold it for $60,000.00. Her dad, Frank gave them a lot on the lake near where he lived. Once while she was gone to Management School in North Carolina, for a week, Heth threw a company party up there for a Saturday picnic, and water skiing, without her knowing it. Their sons stayed with their grandparents while she was gone. She learned that he was very selfish. He cared about getting rich, fishing, and sports. Several men told her that they had noticed how indifferent and disrespectfully her husband treated her.

Heth was baptized twice. She was present each time. Once in Georgia, as a teenager, and once in Peyton Mississippi, in his thirties. The first time it was at a Presbyterian Church, and the second time it was at a Pentecostal Holiness Church of Jesus Christ. In a testimony, which he gave, in his sixties, at a Baptist church, in Georgia, he told that he use to go to the Baptist Church with his grandparents, where he was baptized in the nearby creek, down the road. That simply never happened. He has never lived near there, and has never talked about it. Beulah would know if that happened.

She bought a new, red "American" car, and had an air conditioner installed. This was the first one the company had ever installed. He would go out in the drive way, raise the hood, and undo some of the wiring, so she could not crank it. It was so crazy, because she had not even thought about going anywhere. She only needed to rest and go to church, on weekends.

She had a D & C in 1966, had Endometriosis, and had a Hysterectomy in 1967. On the way home from the hospital Heth said "I guess you will start having sex with other men, now that you can't get pregnant." She responded "you can't get pregnant, do you have sex?" That shut him up. She lost weight down to eighty-seven pounds. Frank told her that he did not worry about her, because she is so stubborn. She remembered that her Gynecologist told her about soldiers of war had to get well enough before the Clergy could reach them or minister to them. Yes, I do know "who I am, a woman who is rich toward God", and I do know "What I am, a child of God".

She filed for divorce in 1968, and paid every penny of it, while he was out of town for two weeks. When he got home, she told him. He got hold of her, twisted her arm, cut her wrist with his watch band, and made her get on the phone and cancel it. He told her that "if she ever tried to divorce him, he would kill her." She had a scar on her right wrist for years. She had already made up her mind that she would attempt to find another man. One way to get divorced was to have an affair (or get fat), and to be sure that the next man would be "SOMEBODY".

Beulah went to her first Seminar, for the Credit Bureau, in South Georgia, for three days. She rode the Greyhound Bus alone. While there, work friends were doing a lot of drinking. She had previously only drunk socially at company parties, with Heth. She over drank and had to ride the bus home. Next morning she had a hangover and could hardly stand or walk. She hurried out to the bus. The doors were locked. She continued to walk up and down, until the driver came and opened the doors for her. That was a long wait. She had to fight sleep; to be sure no one bothered her, while she was in the bus alone.

Moses was a whiz at filing at the office, to help her. Heth wanted to help file. So, she put him to work, but soon sent him home, because he was so slow. It did no good for her to even show him how to sort the files, to speed things up. Also, he spent time looking into people's confidential files. Daniel would not even try to file. It did not interest him.

A friend of Moses called Beulah, at her office, absolutely

frantic. He said that he was pulling Moses (age nine), very fast, on the back of his bike, and they went into a deep ditch and Moses caught his heel in the spokes, and cut it off. Moses had been told repeatedly not to ride double on a bike. The boy was older, bigger boy, and a bully. He had talked Moses into riding with him. However, we did not mention it or bring any charges, because Moses did not obey us. The doctors had to sew layers of stitches to put his heel back together. They had to soak his heel in a gallon of warm water with one cup of Tide washing power in it, for a long time. Moses had to walk on crutches and it took a year for the heel to heal. Moses got very depressed. He still walks with a limp, sometimes.

During the summer of 1965, Beulah attended a Management School, in North Carolina. While standing in line to register, she and another student, business man, could not keep their eyes off each other. They sat together in classes and ate meals together. One night he invited her to his room. Remember that she had never dated. She decided to give it a try. It was dark and they were both fully dressed. While lying on the bed and kissing, he put her hand on his private parts. She soon decided to tell him "I just cannot do this", got up and went out of the room, to her room. That was the end of that friendship.

The second summer she went to Management School, another student, business man, whom she had met the year before, wanted her to go to his room. So, she decided to give it a try. She had no feelings for him, and did not particularly like him. He was a "dud", and she got out of there. He continued to beg her to go, again. After she got home and back to work, she received a letter, at her office, in which he said that he took money out of their saving account to come down to visit her. However, his wife found out about it and he had to spend the money for her a fur coat. Beulah was sure that he was telling a lie. She learned how good and special her husband really was. His problems were in his head.

It took fifty-one years for him to start learning to take the garbage/trash to the road for the dump truck. He would promise to do it, then go straight and get into the car, leave, and not do it. She had to drag two of those large trash cans up the hill to the road.

She set up two websites. Studied, researched, called servers, computer companies, etc., and taught him how to use/publish on the websites for their rental property. He never used them. He could not seem to understand and just did not care. He could not seem to be agreeable about anything. One day she told him "You will always create the same environment, at home, until you change from within". He seemed to take that to heart.

All Beulah's life, she missed very few Sundays, from church. Most of those were when she was sick or had surgery.

He will never have any concept of how wonderful Beulah thought he was, nor how much she loved him. Knowing all that she has learned about men, she would still choose him, when he was sexy, except for the sodomy. He was still the best.

After he Physically held her and made her cancel the divorce, which she had paid for, he said he would agree to have another child. She told him that she would never have another baby by him.

She worked Reader's Digest puzzles, for him. He told people at work that he did them. They told on him. Once after no iron fabrics came on the market, she decided to put a crease in his pants, and slightly iron some of his shirts. She asked how he liked it. He hesitated and said that he could not tell the difference after they were ironed. So, she told him that she would never iron his clothes again. She still hasn't. He did not care if the yard looked like "trash". He was a "hoarder". His barn, his desk, his dresser, and clutter in the house was pathetic.

∞

In 1969 Heth was transferred, by his company, to Peyton, Mississippi. They bought a new, beautiful, red brick, seven room house, with two bathrooms, a carport, small front porch and entrance, and a patio. It was "H" shaped, and located on one and a half acres, in a new housing development. The kitchen and den were unusually large, and one bath room was large enough to put down a double bed, when needed for guest. There was a large fireplace in the den. A row of pines was twenty feet deep crossed the back of the lot.

While settling into the new house at Peyton, MS, Beulah had tailor made, matching drapes and twin bedspreads made, for the Master bedroom. They were so boring that she replaced the bedspreads with her homemade ones.

She had an abundance of fabric scraps, laces, zippers, etc. which Heth had left over from his garment work, and she made most of her clothes.

Shortly after arriving in Peyton, MS, Beulah said that she had been doing music all of her life, and she wanted to do something different. So, she started taking private art lessons, from two different teachers. Within the first year, she had her own Art Studio, in her home and was teaching, ages four to ninety-four, and was teaching in private art stores. She placed a plastic sheet over her new living room carpet and had thirty-six students a week. She was president of the city art club for three years, and a member of the state Art Club. She exhibited over north Mississippi, and parts of Alabama. She painted several murals. She did one for a church festival and one for a Photo Studio. She did art shows in festivals and in cities over North Mississippi, and

Tennessee. Heth traveled with her on Saturdays, and helped set up the tent, and heavy paintings. She judged art for art shows and schools, etc. She went Antiquing in the mountains, with friends. Once a year she and her artist friends chartered a Greyhound bus, and went on a day trip to Memphis, TN on Tours, to visit homes, some of which were movie stars homes. She volunteered to teach art in a nursing home, and ministered in Gospel music at another nursing home there.

The City held a Juried Show. The developer of the project was an attorney. He called Beulah (who was president of the art club) to get names, phone numbers, and addresses of each member. She helped them get the show set up. When it was judged they did not recognize anyone in the art club. Just the director's wife and some of her university classmates won the prizes. His wife drew a "Human ear" in black ink. One meeting Beulah attended an exhibit in a nearby town. The show was to be set up by the same director, at 8:00am and end at 3:00pm. One exhibitor did not show. When 3:00 pm came everyone sat and waited for that one to show up, before they would announce the winner of the prize. Beulah kept saying "well, they have already designated her to get the prize". Surely enough, about 5:00pm there she came. They scurried around to get her three large abstract paintings displayed, and immediately she got the prize money.

In 2002, on their 50th wedding anniversary, their children gave them a Church Wedding. They had gotten married at the county court house, by the Justice of Peace. She had always felt that something was missing, until she had a church wedding.

The average weather was high 97 – 55, and the average low was 24 – 13. It is much more humid in Mississippi than in Georgia.

Grandma Tallie Shiloam died in 1977.

Throughout their two son's growing up, they had many good times camping, just the four of them. Heth would surprise them with Snake Meat for breakfast. Actually it was "Bacon" fried half done, then rolled in flour, and finished frying. They started out camping in a tent, on the coast of North Carolina, camped in the woods of Mississippi, and in camp grounds of Georgia. They bought a popup camper for a few years, then after the boys were out on their own, Heth and Beulah bought a nice rollout camper, and camped in Georgia.

She was a member of a Fort Nightly Music Club. There was a room full of women, all ages, with Music Degrees, and she had not had a music lesson. No one could transpose music for their hymns. She was not familiar with that word "transpose" but she told them that she could move songs to any key they wanted. That she did and the ladies were mystified.

She took swim lessons with her sons at the city pool. Her swim coach was age sixteen. He refused to keep teaching her, because she was afraid of the water. She made excuses. She said she was afraid that her partial tooth would come out. She went home and cried, and Heth laughed at her. She made up her mind to learn to swim, or drown. She ended up learning to swim laps, float, tread water, and dive.

She learned to play bridge and made new bridge friends, at the classes, which the city provided.

She cleaned out Pines in back of the house, tied the Pine needles in sheets and placed them on the sidewalk. People would soon pick them up. Later, she learned how expensive they were for gardening.

Beulah had freckles and her uncle Ryle used to come visit for a week, during the summer, when they were growing up. He told her that she was found under the bridge (the roads were not paved), just above their house, and when it rained mud dripped off under the bridge and fell onto her face. Therefore, the freckles. She grew up thinking that she was ugly, because of the freckles.

In the 1990's she used cream to remove the freckles, and she did not like the way she looked in the mirror. She realized that her freckles did not make her ugly. Rather, they were attractive. Like a Palomino Horse.

She worked as a stenographer for an attorney for a while, typing up court records from cassette tapes. One day he was waiting for her to finish, so he could go to court. When he picked up the records, which she had typed, he noticed that she had spelled "Hind's County" like "Heinz Catsup". He threw a real fit, and everyone in the office came standing around. She flew out of the office and never went back. He blew out of the office and had to make do with her spelling.

When Moses, was age twelve, he was in the Community Theater play. When he was age 17, he was 5'11" tall, weighed 173 and had Auburn Red hair, and beautiful brown eyes. He worked, as assistant manager at Popcorn Stand, in the mall after school and on weekends.

Beulah did a Pastel Mural to go across the back of the stage, for their special program, at church. She spreaded out News Print paper across her large kitchen floor, and invited high school girls to come after school, and help her. It was supposed to represent the 18th century, and she made it for the 19th century, and did not realize it, until that night of the program. That is not the only mistake. The Mural had imprints of the pattern, of the Linoleum on her kitchen floor. But, they all had a great time. Praise God.

Beulah had attended Baptist Missionary meetings all her life. It was time for her to be the host for the upcoming meeting, again. On the meeting day, she cleaned house, arranged chairs, prepared food, and waited for members to arrive. No one showed up. She called the club president, who said the meeting had been changed. They had not let her know. That was the end of Club

Meetings for her. There was not even an apology, to her, for not letting her know.

Heth's dad died, in 1972.

∞

Heth could no longer keep an erection, except to sodomize her. He and a buddy he worked with started going fishing every Saturday morning and staying all day. Finally one day she made a comment about it, and he replied by saying, while smiling a sweet smile, which she had never seen him have before, that his buddy was so sweet and easy to be with. She is certain that she had never heard him talk such sweet talk, to her or anyone else before or since then.

It got to where she would over hear him telling people that he did noteworthy things as if he did them, when in fact she was the one who had done them. He regularly took credit for positive things that she had done.

He quit coming home for lunch, and started eating out. He took her name off of the joint checking account, and said that he would only buy groceries, and that she had to pay for everything else. This was his way of getting the money in savings, which she received in payment of the Credit Bureau, which she sold in Georgia. Therefore, she had to pay for everything – house payments, all insurance, both son's college tuition, etc. This was also his way of making Beulah and the boys pay for all of their education. Both sons had part time jobs, and Daniel made payments on his car. She and the boys had to eat a lot of "Dove". He did a lot of "hunting." In fact one time she started throwing his frozen Dove out of the freezer, until he noticed it and insisted that she stop. A year or so later he announced that he was transferring to North Carolina. She said that she was not going to move with him. He said that he would put her name back on the joint checking account. All of her savings was gone by then. She still said that she was not moving with him. However, he moved her anyway, and left both sons in College on their own.

She began to have visits with the Gastrologist for stomach pains. First visit, he told her that she was afraid that she was going to die. He said that it was caused by her nerves. She told Heth that she did not want to live, and that there was only two reasons that she wants to live, and their names were Daniel and Moses.

He hid money in his shirt and coat pockets in the closet. One time he hid a thousand dollars in an envelope, in the pocket of the automobile. He got started on his trip to take his mama to Georgia, on his way to North Carolina, to work. Well on his way, he remembered to check to see if the money was in the pocket of the car. He could not find it. So, he had to explain to his mama why he was turning around and going back home. He stopped and called Beulah at home and asked if she took the money. She did not know what he was talking about. Later, he called back and said that he had over looked the envelope with the money. It was all there. His mama had made him call and tell Beulah that he found it. She told Beulah about it at a later date.

Beulah was so lonely and upset. Heth worked and did his sports. Their sons were in college, and she felt the pain of how Frank had contributed to her leaving home. When one has a crisis, all previous crises' try to surface. It gets to be overload. Her marrying Heth was a big part, of just a way, of escaping her parents. She wrote three long letters to Frank telling him what she thought about him, about how he thought they were suppose to do everything just like Papa Zech said do it, etc. She mailed one letter a week for three weeks. Farris said that he walked the floors and cried at the store, when he read each one.

In 1975, Beulah burned *in the fireplace*, letters from a suitcase (23" x 18" x 9"), which she had stored in the attic, full of Heth's letters. He had written them during the four years he was in the Navy. They had become like a big joke to her. He wrote her every day, very sweet letters. But, she no longer believed the sweet things he had written to her.

She did not have the one who she married. He committed adultery with his career. He went whoring after riches and fame. His desire was that he wanted to be the president of a large Industrial Company. However, he had relationship problems, and did good to just hold onto a minimal management job.

For the last eight years of his job, he worked off shore. He was so desperate to hold on to his work, and could not accept the fact that he had to retire, that he started communicating with a woman in Angees, SA, doing her spread sheets for her. She kept calling Beulah and asking to speak to Heth. Beulah told her to stop calling and she did a loud, belly laugh. Beulah asked him to put a stop to it. He ignored her. So, she printed out a copy of one of the spread sheets, wrote the president of the company in New York, and mailed it to him. That put a stop to it. That woman had the nerve to say that what Beulah did was unethical.

He had red bumps all over his abdomen (front and back). He said that he asked a doctor to remove them, but the doctor said that he would have to "skin him." A friend, who was in medical school, told her that was caused from too much female hormone (estrogen) in his body.

Any time Beulah uses the word "love", she still thinks about how Frank scolded her when she used the word "love" for material things. He did not know that there are four different kinds of "Love".

Heth worked long hours (15 – 18 hours six days a week), played basketball, with the company team, went fishing with one of his buddies, camped with hunting buddies. He wrecked the boat one summer, but he had it repaired. He quit going to church. The last basketball game he played, for some unknown reason, she decided that she wanted to go with him. About half way through the game, he recovered the ball from a rebound. He turned, started dribbling down the court, at a rapid speed, with all the players following him. She could almost see the halo around his head. Suddenly he tripped, fell flat and hard on his face and belly, with everyone else stumbling over him. It knocked the breath out of him, and took a while for him to recover. She never enjoyed anything so much in all her whole life.

He played golf, always with a handicap score to start with each game. He won seven gold trophies.

She got so tired of Heth using and abusing her, and never showing any affection toward her or Daniel. He gave Moses everything he wanted. Bought him a New, baby blue, Chevrolet to get him to stay in college, and he refused to pay either of their college tuitions. Beulah and the two boys were paying all their college tuition, fees, etc., because he refused to. He never bought a car for Daniel, who had to pay for his own cars. Daniel was always a sweet child to deal with. Both boys were hard workers.

On one occasion, Beulah became so emotionally upset, lonely, and needed someone to communicate with who she thought cared for her. She wrote her oldest sister Drusie about how she just needed someone to pray for her. Drusie wrote her back and told her how sorry she was. Beulah wrote her back and told her "for someone who tries to help people as a Christian, you surely did a good job of putting me down". Beulah would not ever write to her again. That was the only time she had written to her in all the years apart.

It took Beulah years to learn not to love her husband. He was a "touch-me-not". He told her "you act like you can't live without me. I can live without you." By the time he retired she could not tolerate seeing him, or being around him. Since her dad would not let her date, as a teen, she decided to enjoy the affection of other men. One day after an Art meeting, an art friend decided to come over to her house and they tried to have sex on the den couch. But neither could do anything. It was disgusting.

∞

Soon after that she and Heth went to a City Fourth-of-July party and dance. She was age 43, 5', 99lb. 34 bust, 24 waist, and 34 hips. She had on a cute short Ballerina skirt, which her mother-in -law had made for her, as a gift. A well know millionaire, business man asked her to dance. She accepted. After a few minutes, he asked "would you think me presumptuous if I asked you to meet me somewhere." She said "No." He told her where and when to meet him. This was her only affair. After that they met eleven times, once a week. Most of the times at a little farm house, which he owned in their county. A couple of times at another small farm house, which he owned, in a nearby county.

Of all the five men she had been with, she loved two the most. The first and the last. The last one was the oldest, sweetest, and most loving. He was very affectionate, and bought her gifts and said the sweetest things to her.

She saw this as an opportunity to make up for lost time. She knew that she was sinning willfully and would have to pay for her sins, on this earth, that were not under the blood of Jesus. The thing was, she became Agnostic. Actually she was testing God, She had always lived a Christian life, and had no doubts about there being a God or about Jesus His Son, or His Holy Spirit.

After being agnostic for about a year, Beulah asked God for

forgiveness. She told God that she was so sorry, and would give everything back to him, and would do whatever he called her to do. It was worth the lessons she learned. She learned what her husband was and what he was not, or would never be. She had to make up her mind what she really wanted and who she really was. She decided to walk that straight and narrow path. That is when she went into the ministry, and started furthering her education. She always appreciated Heth's hard work, but resented him being such an extremist.

Heth asked her on a late Friday afternoon, in 1977, "Would you like to go to the mall?" She said "yes". When he pulled into the parking space, she opened the door and got out and he drove off and left her. It was about to get dark, so she walked on into the mall. She sat down on a bench about center of the mall. Soon her two sons and their friends came walking by. She told them what happened. They said they would take her home, after a little while. They went on to walk around. After what seemed a long wait, Heth came up smiling very big, and said "would you like a ride home". She did not think it was funny and told him that she had a ride home, and she would not go with him. He left and she rode home with her sons and their friends.

She worked at Department store. One night she had to work until 9:00pm. He was home watching T.V. She called him to come pick her up after work. It was about a two mile drive one way. He refused to pick her up. She had to call a cab and get a ride home. She had never called, or ridden a cab before. Nor had she every ridden alone with a black man (the driver). One day in the fall she became so emotionally upset. They had changed to single beds beside each other, after there was no more sex (except about one in 6-12 months per his choosing), he did find time to sodomize her.

Shortly later, it was rumored at his work, that people thought he was homosexual. His boss called him and the other guy in and told them they had better start showing more attention to their work. It seems that one of the other guy's wives visited Beulah one day and saw the situation. She told the lie/misunderstanding about the two men. Shortly later the other man dropped dead with a heart attack, while coming out of the doctor's office. He had been to the doctor because of pain in his chest and the doctor did not find anything wrong with him.

One Saturday she was having a carport sale. She went into the house and found Heth reading a "porn" magazine, which he had found on the top shelf of their second son's closet. She did not know their son had such a magazine. When Heth saw her coming, he ran and threw the magazine back up on the shelf. She went to see what it was.

One of the few times the four of them ate a meal together, at the supper table, she got sick and was spitting up mucus. He told their sons that she was drunk. She had only one drink of Jack Daniels. She only went to a liquor store once in her life. Later, she told her parents about going into a store, where the clerk asked how old she was and would not believe how old she was. Frank started picking her about the store. She just ignored him. The clerk was sure that Beulah was not eighteen. Actually she was in her 40's.

One evening the four of them were in the large den. Both of the boys were home from college for the weekend. Heth was in the kitchen sharpening his knife. She was rocking in front of the fireplace. Suddenly he started coming at her while still sharpening the knife. She felt with all of her being that he was planning to stab her. She snarled up her face and braced herself. She planned if he did, to kick him backwards. He just calmed down and walked calmly on by. They did not communicate about that at all.

One evening Heth went wild. He started looking through kitchen cabinet doors, slamming them, and did not know what he was looking for.

Early one morning Wolly Parks came to the door. He said that he was going to live with Mrs. Ross. She told him "Wolly" you are going to get on the phone and ask your mother if you can live with Mrs. Ross. He did and she said "yes. He had taken his mother's car, driven it from Georgia to Miss (driving all night). She had reported the car stolen, and had police looking for him all across the country. It was his and Daniels senior years, in high school. Beulah and Heth started both of them to college, together. He went on to be an Attorney, and Daniel spent thirty-three years in the U.S. Army. Wolly and his family: mother, dad, and three brothers lived across the street from Beulah's. They moved there about the same time. Wolly always said "Daniel is my brother"…"Daniel is my brother". Wolly's dad had died suddenly, early one morning while still in bed. His heart ruptured. His mother took him and his youngest brother to Georgia to live with relatives.

Wolly Parks was standing around in the kitchen, one afternoon, looking very pensive, while Beulah was making a gallon of Tea. After a while he said "you know, Mrs. Ross, I bet someday they will pipe Tea to people's houses". She replied "I am the one to do it…I am the one to do it….." She had to make tea frequently for her sons and their friends.

CHAPTER SIX

MAKING THE ROUNDS

Jam. 3:14 But, if you have bitter envying, and strife in your hearts, glory not. KJV

He had moved her (against her will) to Waynes, NC. This was a little country girl moved to a large city in 1981. It was a new, split level house, bricked up part of the way and white, wood siding the rest of the way up. The stairs entry carried you into the open living room, dining room, and kitchen. Down the hall west, was the first bathroom on the right. Across the hall was a bedroom that served as a Den. In the left back corner was the guest bedroom, and across from it was the master bedroom, with the on suite bathroom. Back down stairs was her art room, and a large Den with a large fireplace. To the west of that was the double garage.

One cold winter Sunday, they sat in front of the large fireplace, with the gorgeous open fire, watching Television. He glued Moth holes, all over a green suit which he did not like and only wore a few times. Of course, he never wore it again. At least he was occupied for a few hours.

Heth left to go to work one morning, and forgot to open the automatic garage door. He backed into the double door, and tore both of them enough that they had to be replaced.

One morning she was playing the piano when he kissed her "good bye" and she was still playing when he returned for lunch and kissed her "hello". She had played five hours without stopping, and did not realize what time it was. The weather in North Caroline was a little cooler than in Georgia, by a few degrees.

Beulah, Heth, Daniel, and Moses were all work-a-holics.

They, Mandy, and Mark Hailers and their children (they had four – one boy, and three girls) use to spend many hours together. Both were an only child in their family, and were spoiled. They were pitiful, because they had no relatives. They had not been taught work ethics, etc. They and their children picked up rocks and helped clear land for a Golf Course. They use to spend Sunday afternoons there. That is where Beulah first ate Ritz Crackers with Cream Cheese on them. She must have eaten half the box, in one afternoon. She was ashamed of herself. They moved into an old, small farm house in the country, with only well water. Beulah, Heth and boys use to go out there on weekends, and party just their two families. They treated Beulah and family like relatives, because they had none. They met in church, in Marlo, NC, and attended the same church together in Waynes, NC for years.

In 1982, while he was gone out of town, for three weeks, out of town, on a company trip, She just quit eating and only drank a few sips of Diet Pepsi each day. She lost down to eighty-seven pounds. She fell sick. While standing at the sink washing dishes, her bottom began to shake, and she fell to the kitchen floor. She could not call him, he would not allow that, and he always refused to call home to check on her and or the boys, when he went out of town. She gradually crawled to the phone and called a neighbor whom she did not know. She looked up the phone number by the address. They lived across the street. The man agreed to come over and get her and take her to the emergency room. The doctors checked her in with heart problems (Mitral Valve Prolapse). She stayed in the hospital for a week and no one else knew that she was there.

After a week, when it was time for Heth to return home, she called him and told him to come after her, which he did. As usual nothing was said about the incident. He cannot be reasoned with. The doctors said she might have had a stroke. They did not say for sure. Her heart doctor put her in Rehab for six weeks. She took swim lessons as part of her therapy. She got him to sign an consent form, for her to take swim lessons, with her friend, the doctor's wife,and she learned to lap swim.

While in rehab, the Nutritionist ran blood test on everything that she normally ate, and found out that she was allergic to almost all of them. They made her heart beat too fast.

After she got out of the hospital, Frank found out through Heth's mother (who was neighbor to her parents), that she had been in the hospital for a week, with a heart problem. She called her parents. Frank immediately called her, at night, and told her that he had the same heart problem, and so did his mother. She died at age 96, and he died at age 88. He asked her if things could just be like they use to be (between him and her). She said "Yes". From then forward, nothing was ever mentioned about what happened. He did not apologize for running her off.

Her parents had been listening to a preacher, on Television, who preached and sold materials on British Isralism, which is a cult. They had ordered a study course from him. They believed that the United States and Great Britain were the two lost tribes of Israel.

A few months earlier her dad had disowned her. So, she could not call home. What happened was, during a cold spell in February, per her request, Heth had taken her to stay with both her parents and cook for them. They were bed ridden. First night she was there he was talking about who Israel was. He is a bible fanatic. He made the remark that those returning to Israel, were not Israelites. She asked "who do you think they are". He blew up with one of his Shiloam fits, told her to leave and it was 10:30pm. She did not know what to do. It was a four hour drive to where she and Heth lived. Therefore, she just went to the back room and went to bed. Next morning she called Heth's sister Joy to come get her. She came and got her and all of her belongings and carried her to her home for the rest of the week. They had a wonderful time. Her husband was Beulah's second cousin, and they both were very welcoming she went to church with Joy. She showed her how to play the piano, and they cooked. While she was there Cassie called and told Beulah that Frank did not mean what he said. She insisted that Beulah come back home. However, Beulah hung up on her. She called Heth, at the end of the week, and he came after her.

After Beulah returned home, she noticed that she could hardly see out of her left eye. She called her heart doctor. He told her they thought she might have had a stroke, but never would confirm it. He made her an appointment in Roach, NC, with an eye Specialist. They found that she had three white (dead) spots in that eye, and was legally blind. They gave her a black patch. clip on, to attach to her glasses, but she would not wear it after a while. After a few weeks, she was reading a magazine from Gloria and Kenneth Copland and began to see. Not perfectly, but enough to read, without her glasses.

She called her pastor, and he asked her to testify the following Sunday morning instead of having preaching, he asked her to come up and give her testimony. She did, and he asked her to stay on stage. He asked everyone who needed healing for their eyes to come up front. A large line came. He and she laid hands on those who came for healing in their eyes.

Heth sat back about middle ways of the church, and people around him told her that he cried through the whole service. After church people asked her if she knew there was a light shown around her face, as she testified. She did not know that. Heth told her that he saw it.

That night during the night service, the pastor asked all who had healings in their eyes, that morning, to come up front and lineup. There were twenty nine people who came.

Later the pastor asked Beulah to go to Burls, NC to give her testimony on the new Christian Television Station. She did. Therefore, numerous people were healed. Soon she visited a new large shopping center, in the same town, and several people stopped her and told her that they received healing in their eyes, while watching her Television testimony.

In June 1981 she had surgery on her left elbow to remove a bone knot, and repaired and shortened a tendon, which had been stretched through use. Most likely because of playing octaves on the piano.

She had two surgeries on top of her head/scalp, about one inch long, in the center of her head, for Basel Cell Carcinoma cancer. Doctors did not get it all first surgery. During the second surgery, she had an allergy/seizure. They put her in a bed with bars all around it. They called in two heart doctors' et al. After a while the jerking subsided.

∞

Both worked with the deaf & blind. They studied Spanish language, and sign language at the Community College. She did volunteer work at a summer camp for the deaf,

There was nothing humble about Frank or Heth. Both were filled with pride and would never admit their faults or mistakes.

Their first grandchild was born December 1982. She weighed

eight pounds, was bald headed, and had beautiful blue eyes. As her hair grew[1] it was blonde and curly.

Heth was very hostile to Beulah the whole time they lived there. One day they started out to get into the car, to go somewhere. She made a remark about such muddy tires on his vehicle. She asked him where he got the mud. He worked in a large city with paved streets. He told her "it was where they were working on the street, on his way to and from work." He lies so much, he must think that she does not have any more sense than he does. She responded "that could not do that much mud." She had seen the streets they were working on. She knew that was not true, but did not dare to respond.

A few weeks later, a work and hunting buddy, of Heth's brought his wife with him, to visit them. The four of them had been friends in Georgia. She and Beulah sat in the back yard, under a shade tree. During the conversation, her friend mentioned that her husband told about how Heth said, that he had to sneak out of the house, a few weeks earlier, with his hunting clothes, because Beulah would not let him go hunting. Beulah said "I don't know what you are talking about. He never mentioned anything to me about wanting to go hunting." Beulah said "that explains why he came home with mud all over the tires and slung all around the vehicle.

He and Beulah were not communicating at that time. (Sometimes they went for months, without communicating because he would not tell the truth or could not comprehend.) Heth is such a habitual liar. He does not seem to know the difference between the truth and a lie. God's word says in Revelations that, there will be no liars in heaven, and other places in the bible it states that God hates a "lie".

It was a cold fall night, Heth returned home from work after midnight. He would not speak..He went to the guest room, turned down the bedspread, and crawled in it. There were no sheets or pillow cases on the bed. There was nothing for her to do, but go to bed in their master bedroom. He still has never mentioned what happened that night or why he was so late returning home. She knew that he was suppose to have worked in a nearby town, at the plant. He and the plant manager there did not get alone very well. The plant manager would not do what Heth said. Later that guy got him back when he became manager of the plant where Heth worked. He fired Heth. They had a brawl.

Heth's position was what she called "a snooper". He went to plants and checked the work, oversaw the equipment, and measured fabric, up to a sixty-fourth of an inch, or more. He worked alone.

One morning he left his office, laid his work papers on the top of his vehicle, and forgot about them. He took off down the four lane highway and they scattered all different directions. He had to get out and pick them up among all the traffic.

She learned in her teens that she had the gift of giving, and was altruistic. She learned in the 1920's that she was an Extravert, in the 1950's that she was Choleric, and was always empathetic.

They did not speak to each other, except when necessary. He was angry about something. One day at lunch he got up from the table and threw his plate of food cross the room and it landed on the Refrigerator, with food scattered around the kitchen floor. It stayed there, until he cleaned it up five weeks. Later. Of course, it was dried hard by them. She refused to touch it and walked around it, daily.

∞

In 1986-2000, she wrote five poems, which were published in hardback, by the National Library of Poetry. She also was named in "Who Is Who Of America".

While visiting an old friend, she introduced Beulah to her friend, and told her, that Beulah was a pianist. The other girl was a student at the Junior College. She replied with a smart mouth "she must be very frustrated". She had recently taken a course in Psychology, from a secular school, and wanted to show her smarts. They interpret talent as frustration. I believe most mental illnesses are evil spirits Jesus never made any exceptions for the mental illnesses. The bible does speak to "anger, jealousy, drinking alcoholic beverages, and gluttony, etc. I know for a fact that some people can have head or brain damage, or some other physical damage, that causes them to not act or talk normal and can alter their behavior. The bible gives healing scripture for every mental disorder and what to do to be healed from physical disorders.

It was early, on a cold February morning, while traveling on a business trip, with her husband, she had her make-up in a tool box. When she got into an elevator, several business men were in there. One man asked if she was going fishing? She told him "No this is my make-up box". It was not long until pink, fancy little boxes, similar to a tool box, were on shelves and young girls were buying them, like hot cakes.

In 1980's Heth traveled flew to E Paso, Texas frequently for a week to work. She flew with him. Once while in that area, they went to Waras, Mexico, for four days. She said, when they left, that she would never go out of the U.S., again.

Beulah had no formal music training, but she was self taught along with her mother had Taught her to read notes and time. However, she loved to play by ear all over the piano. She could hear something and then play it. One friend use to say that if a piano had a thousand notes, Beulah would have to hit everyone of them. She went weekly, to several Nursing Homes, in the area, and ministered in Gospel Music, playing piano, key board, and singing.

Both studied Spanish at the Community College. They

studied sign language and worked with deaf and blind. They were members of a "Club for The Deaf." One summer she worked at a camp for the deaf. When the club needed a volunteer for the position of President, they asked Beulah and she declined. Then, Heth came alone and volunteered for the Presidency. Now, Heth worked from 6:00am until 10:00pm six days a week, Beulah has to deal with all business, cut the grass or hire it cut, and get all the yard work done. The boys were both in College in Mississippi. He will not do anything at home. He is above all that. He thinks that all he is responsible for is going to work. She has tried, begged, and cried for thirty years for him to take the heavy garbage cans to the road. He will promise to do it, but gets right into the car and drives off. He has never held an office except Scout Master, when the boys were growing up, except the deaf club had started the Halloween project, whereby, they had to work nights to build props. That is what he wanted to do. So, she did not complain.

She started to a Pentecostal Holiness Church, with a neighbor. While living there, she watched a lot of Oral Robert's, and other Charismatic evangelist, on Television, as well as read many books/magazines relating to the scriptures. Also, she went to school on line, to Woodrow University, graduating from Bible College, before the University had been accredited. After they were accredited. She received a BS de3gree in Church ministry and Christian Education. Then, she received a MA degree in Counseling and Christian Psychology, and a minor in Psychology. She studied and painted watercolors, in the Motel rooms, while Heth was working out of town. She also, went to three different Nursing homes and ministered in Music, weekly.

She found beads of blood; on the beige carpet; in the bathroom, while living in Waynes, North Carolina. He denied it. He said that their sons did it. But no one else had been in the room. Their sons lived in Mississippi, and she had her own bathroom. He refused to go to a doctor.

For Christmas 1981, Beulah told Heth that she wanted a bottle of Chanel # 5 for her Christmas gift. He bought a bottle of Chanel # 5 and another kind of Perfume, and gave the Chanel # 5 to his Secretary and the other Perfume to Beulah. He is so manipulative and hateful.

They helped start a new, large Baptist Church. They asked her to sketch a picture of the new church for the program, on Dedication Sunday. She did it for free. The preacher came to see her before it was published and told her the windows were too small and they look like a prison . She looked at it and agreed. He offered to get someone else to do it over. She insisted "no" that she could do it correctly. She explained that happens with artist, sometimes, they get so close to their work, they can't view it naturally. One has to stand back and view their work, or they lose perspective. Therefore, she redid the windows and it was printed. He said "that is what happens to my sermons, sometimes".

She was organist at the Alliance Church, located down the street, in walking distance. Twice she attended a Retreat at a Resort, in North Carolina, with the church missionary lady's group. First time she went, she was so disappointed, because most of the women there from other cities, including their group, were so silly and acted like third graders. They acted like they had never been away from home, before. One group from a certain church, were the most extreme. The preacher's wife was a big part of the foolishness. Her dad liked to act silly/funny, and that is how she learned to act. Some greased doorknobs during the late night. Some hung wallpaper over elderly ladies door, during the wee hours of the night. Second time she went with the group, she tacked a cardboard sign outside her door, with scriptures (mostly from Proverbs) related to foolishness, folly, and idle words. Whew, that really set off a "storm". They ganged up, and her preacher's wife led them to knock on her door early, next morning. They wanted to know why she did it. The group who was had the worse behavior the year before, was sure that the scriptures were pointing out them. BIT DOG HOLLERS! She told them she did it, because God laid it on her heart to do it. So, they left.

By 1980, Beulah had known who she was in Christ – "a child of God." She also knew where she was going to live eternally with her heavenly Father and Jesus. She knew God and His Son Jesus (John 17:3).

There are five stages of Grief: Denial, Anger, Blaming, Depression, and acceptance. These are the usual stages a person goes through in grief. Some may go through each in this order. However, sometimes people get hung up in one or more stages, and need help to move on, with grief. If one remains in one or more stages, of grief, for six months or longer, they need professional help. Beulah's grief centered, mostly on whether Heth was saved. His life did not always reflect salvation. She finally had to just give it to God, and turn it a loose.

∞

In 1964 they moved to Mica, Georgia for the first time.

The house there was a small, two bed room, one bath with a living room, kitchen, and carport, on a circle with local housing, and a highway running along the back of the 1 acre lot. There was a triple row of Pines on the west side of the house. It had a black Shingle roof. After a year of her having the income from the Credit Bureau and Collection agency they could now afford to close in the carport, on the east side of the house, and make a den, fixing a bar between the kitchen and the den, with a two step down. The utility room became a large brick fireplace, with a beautiful mantle. On the other end of the house, they built a large bedroom, with a long bath. They bought a utility room building to place out back for their junk, moved from the old utility room.

They attended the Church of God, where Beulah was pianist and worked with the elderly. They participated in a healing service there, one night of revival. A middle aged lady had a brace on her left leg and she came down for prayer saying the doctors said she had Osteoporosis. The church gathered around her. A young man (who had only been in the church for three weeks) asked her to sit on the front bench and take the brace off of her leg, which she did. He stooped down and held her heel in his hand, and they began to pray. Then a miracle happened. They watched her left leg grow out as long as her right leg. No one had noticed that she had one leg shorter than the other. She jumped up and started running around the church, praising the Lord. She then stood up and while they were praising the Lord, she asked for more prayer. She fell forward, slain in the spirit, and the lady minister said "she has an evil spirit; some of you pray that demons will not tear or hurt her, while the rest of us pray for her". The spirits began to manifest. The preacher would ask what their names were, one at a time, as they manifested. They cast out eleven evil spirits. They were rebellious and would growl, speak mean things through the lady, but as they all prayed in Jesus' name, commanding each one, they had to come out. They gave their names as "incest, sexual abuse, adultery, anger,etc." She became a totally different person after that experience, in her behavior and even the way she dressed, later. The carpet was wet and they used nearly a whole roll of paper towels from where she spit up after each evil spirit came out.

Heth had ear surgery to repair an ear drum, which he damaged while water skiing.

Their second granddaughter was born in May 1986, weighing 10 lbs. She had beautiful blue eyes, and was bald headed. As her hair grew, it was blond and curly.

∞

In just six months after they moved to Mica, Georgia, the second time, and bought a beautiful house, Heth was transferred to Scars', Mississippi, in 1986.

The house was a beautiful yellow brick with nine large windows across the front. It was on a circle, in a new housing development. They built a swimming pool, in back of the patio, which took a lot of grading to level the yard for the pool. It was four bedrooms, three baths, a living room, dining room, kitchen, had a front foyer, and a double carport. They built a Pool House, and storage house on the east side of the pool and house. There was a wooded area on the east side of the yard. The lot was two acres. They set out shrubbery in the front yard, and made a flower bed. The yard sloped down from the road to the back of the lot.

While there, she was ordained and licensed to preach and minister. She founded and pastured a Pentecostal Holiness International Church, and had a fifteen minute radio sermon, five days a week, on the local station, for five years.

Heth got up and went to work early and let her sleep. As soon as they got settled in, a man (sounded like a large, black man) called Beulah and woke her up, every morning around six o'clock. She would hang up. Later she started telling him to "stop calling her and waking her up". Finally after several months, one morning she told him "What do you want". He responded "I want you to meet me at such and such store". She asked where it was located. He explained directions. She asked "what time". He told her. She said "okay", and hung up. He never called again.

They bought a new, Navy Blue Buick, then he got into a fight with the plant manager, who tried to fire him, and he would not quit. He still went to work every morning for several days. Then, he finally gave up the fight and found a job with the Census Bureau for about six months.

After months of searching for an Industrial job, he found one and they moved to Hastens, South Carolina, where he worked as plant manager.

The house was a new, two story, in a new housing development. The outside was a blue/grey pickled finish (oil base stain). Shrubbery and flower beds were already set out. It had a winding stairs just inside the front foyer, a living room to the left (west), a dining room to the north, a kitchen back of the front foyer, a half bath to the east of the dining room, and a pantry at the back of the kitchen. South, outside the kitchen was a patio. From the kitchen front/east was a door to the double garage. Upstairs was three bedrooms and a bath.

While they were attending a company Christmas party, everyone was seated around the tables. After a brief conversation, his boss looked at Heth and said "Heth, you married above yourself". Heth replied "I know, but she chose me".

Cassie said in the 80's that she was going to talk to brother Todd's wife about getting too fat, and eating too much. Beulah laughed and told her that she was not going to do it, because she remembers the time when Cassie was fat and she hated it as much as anyone, but could not lose weight. She was still over weight at the time she made the remark. Cassie did not respond. She just looked angry.

When Beulah obtained the job in Celest, SC, working with 95% blacks, and started the church in Raines, MS (including her own daily radio programs, and teaching in black schools 65%

black), her heart filled with joy. She felt that she had fulfilled her calling to minister to blacks.

It was a few years later, when she was organist and Church Psychologist for a Pentecostal Holiness Church, they needed a new secretary. Therefore they requested that Beulah be the secretary. She declined. Heth then volunteered for the position. She knew what he would do, take the position and Beulah would have to do the work. So, she told the church what he was doing and said that this was not the first time he had pulled this trick. She told them that she would resign as organist if they gave him the job. She was in school (on-line) and was too busy to do the job for him. The church tabled the nomination and they never heard any more about it. He did this for the Deaf and Blind Club and served one year.

Having studied Psychology since 1979, Beulah was able to figure out that Heth was an Introvert, had a Melancholic, Phlegmatic Personality and was Schizophrenic. At this point in life, it stands to reason that, Beulah would come to learn that Frank's Shiloam fits were actually "Bipolar" manifestations (episodes of Mania), Narcissistic, and Sanguine Personality. Not to mention, her own diagnosis was Choleric Personality, Extravert, with an IQ of 168. Then, there was her mother Cassie, who was (according to her diagnosis) Phlegmatic, Agoraphobic, and an Introvert.

CHAPTER SEVEN

MENTAL HEALTH

Acts 20:27 .....to declare unto you all the counsel of God. KJV

W hen Heth was Scout Master in Mica, Georgia, he made a wool blanket for the boy scouts to present it to the best behaved boy, at the next camp. Beulah knew that he would find some excuse to not give it to anyone, and would keep it for himself. (SHE KNEW HIM!). He made it from scraps, which he had left over from his job. Sure enough. When they returned from camp, he told her that he did not give the blanket to any one, because they all misbehaved.

She was saved in 1945, and raised in the Southern Baptist Church. However, the Lord brought her into the Pentecostal Holiness Church in 1980. Her expertise has always been Gospel Music, with years in the Gospel Music Ministry.

While both of them were without a job, in Hastings, SC, they were applying for jobs, she was finishing her Master's Degree in Psychology, and he was still looking for Garment Industrial work. They agreed that whoever got a job first, that is where they would move.

She found a job with the Mental Health Department in Celest, SC. He helped move her there, bought her a new T.V., built her a kitchen cabinet, did everything she needed. However, he refused to move to that small town. He felt there was nothing there for him.

She had her own office and worked as a Counselor/Therapist. Population there was ninety-five percent Black. Her home office, where she was hired and had to drive to weekly meetings was in Carol, SC, about fourteen miles from her office. In 1993 it ranked as the number one city in the U. S. with the worst crime record. On several occasions she had to drive a van full of patients to other cities to go shopping, etc. She was assigned to suicidal patients, in a hospital, in another city. She had to visit patients who were disabled locally.

While she worked there, Heth lived with their son Moses, in Tennessee, for one year, and worked for him, in his Research Business.

Beulah became her own person, a real person, and an individual,. She knew who she was for the first time, in her life She decided what she would do and not do, or believe. In the past she had always done what per parents, and husband said or wanted. Now she could make her decisions, go, do, what she wanted. She decided that she liked who she was, and she would have a changed life.

While working- there, the state of South Carolina did not allow employees to talk with patients about the bible, or Christianity. She learned, in listening to clients, who came with their tales about how their pastors would only tell them to "pray" about their problems. Clients did not even know scriptures well enough to council with them. She could give them one or two scripture verses and they felt relieved.

One of her clients was an elderly man, who had "Tuberculoses. All of the other counselors refused to take him. So, the manager assigned him to Beulah. She did not know that you could catch

T.B. by breathing the air they had breathed. Soon after, the state required each employee to take a T.B. inoculation. Beulah's showed up positive, but dormant.

One Friday night he called her and said that he was coming to spend the week end. She was so upset, because she had a hard work week and needed rest. They sat out on the screened in porch, and he talked constantly, until midnight. She did not respond much, because she mostly slept.

Beulah visited her aunt Phyllis Woodall who lived on route to her parent's, where she drove home on weekends. One day she told Phyllis that, as a teen she remembered hearing Cassie say "When I moved back with him (to Georgia), I said that I would never leave him (Frank) again." Beulah had been curious if she remembered correctly that at one time her parents were separated. Phyllis said "I think that you remember right".

As no surprise, in 1992 Heth lost his job, again. He found another job in the garment industry, in Niles, Georgia, which only lasted about six months.

After several months, he finally found a job in Hastin Mfg, Trillon, Georgia. They rented out their house in Hastings, SC to a young man, who was the choir director at the first Baptist Church. He kept defaulting on the rent. Therefore, they were preparing to take him to court. When they would call him about payments, he just laughed at them. Months later he said that he would get the payment from his mother. A few weeks later, they received a check from her for the full amount, and evicted him. Heth moved into an apartment in Trillon, Ga. He would visit Beulah on some weekends. One time he forgot to take any money with him. He had only the change in his pocket. Next time he visited her he told her about he bought a pack of Nabs crackers, and a few apples. She could not imagine him not calling her to wire him some money.

Beulah's middle sister, Farris, had an Aneurism, in 1990, in the same place, where she hit her head, on the rod of a plow, on the tractor, when she was age four. Frank was letting her ride on his new tractor while he was trying it out. The doctors could not do surgery. So, they clamped the Aneurism off, and told the family that she would not live more than five years. She has lived 26 years and has had three pacemakers in the last fifteen years. Frank blamed himself for her falling on the tractor. Beulah consoled him by telling her she could have been born with a weak place there, or the Aneurism could have been caused from another injury. Aunt Reba said that the time Farris hid under the bed and cut her hair over the right eye, in the same place, was an "Omen". She almost did not have any hair, when she was a toddler. She had been lost for a good while, and we could not find her. She came crawling out from under the bed with the scissors and her hair cut.

She had a professional job, before the aneurism, but after that she was declared incompetent, and unable to work at public work. However, she cuts tree limbs, and trims bushes in relatives and neighbor's yards, without consent, not to mention all the other things she feels privileged to do. No one can do anything with her. Her son and daughter live out of state and Beulah is stuck to deal with her. She has killed trees and bushes by cutting them down, or over fertilizing them, in Beulah's yard

That is not the worst thing she does. She has always been very jealous of Beulah and wants to look just like her. If Beulah even mentions what she will wear and coloring her hair, next time they go somewhere, she shows up looking just like Beulah.

Heth found a job in Strain, MS, in 1994. He and Mosses insisted that she should give up her job. But, she reluctantly moved with him, for six months. He went to work at 6:00am and came home at 9:00pm, ate supper, then went to work on the computer until 1:00pm every night. Therefore, she talked him into buying a house in Strain, one mile from their oldest son Daniel and his family. So, they moved there. He kept an apartment in Strains, where he worked and drove him to Strains on weekends, for six years.

The weather there was high 102 – 57, and the low was 26 - - minus 2 degrees. It was extremely humid, during the summers. They spent a lot of time on the lake water skiing.

The house there was a split level, red brick, four bedrooms (two upstairs and two downstairs), three baths, living room, dining room, and a large den with a large fireplace and a raised hearth. Her Art Studio was in the north half of the basement. There was a patio in the back yard, with a high stairs entrance, because of the hill about half way across the yard. The back yard was wood fenced, with a flower garden inside and outside, next to the fence. There was a cement patio off the den, on the east side.

Heth had two inches of his colon removed. Third day he was home, he could not urinate. His abdomen looked like he was six months pregnant. He would not let her call 911. When he got to where he could not walk, she called his doctor. They sent out an ambulance. They had to pick him up and put him on the Stretcher, to put him in the ambulance. About a year later he had a Hernia on his left lower abdomen. They had to insert a "mesh."

Beulah Founded a Pentecostal Holiness Church, in Raines, Mississippi, and pastured there for eight years. Beulah did fifteen minute sermons, and one minute, sermons on radio, five days a week. She did editorials in the local newspaper. Population there was sixty-four percent Blacks. Therefore, their church membership was mostly Blacks, except for her and Heth. The Pentecostal Church was the first denomination to accept women as pastors.

There was one Pastor, who Beulah recognized as having an Incest relationship with his 20 year old daughter. She prayed that God would put a stop to the relationship, speedily. Three weeks later his heart burst, and he died instantly.

One Black man in the church was literally a giant. He and two other Black men joined the church requesting to be baptised. Since the church rented and did not have a Baptismal Pool. They had to figure out where to have a Baptismal service. Beulah was a member of the YMCA and swam there weekly. So, she planned for the men to meet her there on a Wednesday. When the men arrived, she directed them down stairs, to the dressing room. As she turned to go to her dressing room, the manager, et al behind the desk, asked what they were doing. She explained and the manager graciously said "who are we to stand against the work of the Lord". Thus, we met and went into the water. She soon learned that she could not hold the men up to baptize them. Therefore, she asked the assistant pastor and another member to actually do the process of Baptising.

Two Black preachers, who were originally from Raines, MS, joined the church. They wanted controlling positions in the church, and even requested that the church give them a car. They got offended when Beulah refused both, and they soon left.

While living there, Beulah studied by mail, from the University & Seminary, in Indiana, from 1997 until 2001. That is where she received half of her Doctorate Degree in Theology. Again, when he worked out of town, she frequently, studied while sitting in motels.

Beulah was a Substitute School Teacher in the Mississippi School System. She taught in all subjects, in grades K – 12. 1994-1998. She retired in August of 1998. She frequently taught Special Ed.

While living in Raines. Beulah was one of the Hosts/Guides, for the Russian Expo, "Splendors of VERSAILLES", which visited

Mississippi, in Derdon, for three months. She and several friends commuted week days. As it was closing, the city gave a banquet for the Hosts, it was huge and awesome. Beulah had poison oak broke out on her chin, about the size of a nickel. Sitting there in her formal attire, during the meal, it was oozing into her plate. She kept saying "Something is falling from the ceiling into my plate", until she figured out what it was. People around did not comment. They just stared.

When traveling, Heth would not stop to use the bathroom, until he needed to gas up, no matter how much she begged. She got to where she would take an empty coffee can with a lid, sit in the back seat and urinate while traveling. Once, Beulah was traveling with Heth to Louisiana, for a week, to work. He had driven for one and a half hours, when she told him that she did not want to go. He turned around and carried her back home.

In 1996 While counseling with a client, who was going through a divorce, the lady said that her husband was a "non-person". After she described him, Beulah thought "hm-m-m that is what Heth, Cassie, and Drusie are".

Cassie died in her sleep, at age 84, with heart failure. She had a stroke six years previously. She was two years older than Frank.

Beulah joined a Garden Club of all elderly ladies. They thought that since she had a new van, that she was suppose to transport them to whatever events they wanted to attend, of course. There was on old lady who told most everyone what to do and was very controlling. They did not ask her to drive. When she showed up to go with them, they told her that she was driving. She soon quit the club. It was disgusting how they controlled her. She was their newest and youngest member.

In 1997 Heth had Alzheimer and Prostrate Problems. He refused to talk or discuss things. If something was important enough. She wrote notes/letters to him. He always responded with lies, confusion, twisted words, things that were not true. There was no making sense with him. If I did something noteworthy, he told people that he did it. Communicating became progressively more/totally impossible, as the years went by. She spent years crying and praying that Heth could change, become loving/lovable, until she gave up and became agnostic. That is when she had an affair, which lasted three months.

One rainy, Sunday afternoon, while Heth was doing 1998 taxes, Heth got angry and jut pouted. He would not talk. Beulah finally picked it out of him. He said that because she worked, it put him in a higher tax bracket. She told him that she would pay her taxes on what she made. Later, she noticed that he had charged her almost all the whole amount of taxes, which he had made, for the year. He admitted that he charged her for his taxes, too. She gave him a check for only her amount of the taxes, and it was not mentioned again.

She learned that he was a millionaire, in 1998. All those years he had her and the boys scrimping and pinching pennies, he was having large sums taken out of every pay check, to deposit to his savings. The way she found out was, that she called a Finance Company to find out what their interest rates were, and he began trying to sell her some business. When she told him about the accounts they already had, he told her that they needed to have a Revocable Trust set up, and he set up an appointment with an attorney to talk with them.

In 1998, She had four surgeries on her left eye, for Basil Cell Carcinoma Cancer, at the Hospital in Derdon, MS.

Beulah had a facelift, then a partial face lift, in 1998. Later she had six face precancers removed. At age sixty-five, you would swear that she was no more than 40 years old, by looking at her. She was five feet tall, and weighed ninety-eight pounds. She had always looked younger than her age.

Beulah began putting together her biography. Also, she started a book of her sermons, which her oldest granddaughter Sheila Shiloam typed for her. Beulah paid her by the hour to work after school and on weekends. She felt that Sheila needed to understand that Christianity is not funneled down through a male priest, since Jesus arose. Sheila and her sister Gloria attended a Catholic school, and Beulah paid the tuition. Sheila was born on Beulah's birthday, and she stayed in the clouds for three months. It was her first grandchild.

Beulah had prophesied about Frank years earlier, in 1994, she said that they would watch him suffer for his sins, if he was a true Christian. The bible teaches that any sins not under the blood of Jesus Christ will be paid for, here on earth, if a person is saved. She had told Frank, years ago, that he was called to preach. He responded that he knew it. But he just could not do it. She responded "well none of us can do anything without God. If He calls us, he will provide what we need for every occasion". His body was riddled with Arthritis. He had walked with a cane, then crutches under both arms, and he had a stroke and lay in bed for fifteen or more years, flat of his back. He was a hypocrite, preached to everyone, hanged hand written scripture verses, on cardboard, all over this store/service station. He was dogmatic, and opinionated. It is a fearful thing to fall into the hands of the Lord. Hebrews 10:31.

Beulah rarely dreamed about her future. She just lived in the present, one day at a time. All she cared about was to have peace, and joy in Christ. She didn't care if she lived in a log cabin, down on the river. She felt called at age twelve to be a missionary, when she was growing up. After marriage she dreamed of retirement, with Heth, when she built "air castles" Frank called them.

One weekend they were traveling on the four lane interstate, approaching Birmingham, Alabama, when the car gave out of gas. As it chugged to a stop, Heth pulled it off on a ramp. She sat in the car, alone, while he walked unknown miles to get gas.

When Heth was living alone in an apartment in Strain, MS, he usually came home every week end. However, he packed his clothes and left with the attitude that he was never coming back. Later in the week he called and said that he was coming home for the week end. She was surprised. He came home, acted very romantic, hugging, kissing, and pretended to want sex, which he tried, then left. A few days later, when she had a cold and the itchy "Crabs" on her private parts, she figured out that he came home to intentionally give her a bad cold and the "Crabs". When she confronted him about it, he did not deny it, but would not say that he was sorry.

While he worked off shore, he would call on Sundays. However, he failed to call one Sunday. So, she called his boss and told him, that she had not heard from him. His boss had someone locate him and call Beulah. Heth said that he was watching a movie with some friends, whom he had invited to his hotel room, and he forgot to call her. She knew he had a girl friend. Every time he called in the evenings someone would knock on his hotel door and she heard him invite a lady in. He said it was a maid between 7:00pm and 8:00pm. She told him that she did not believe him. Later she asked her two sons if they believed that and they said "No."

After that she refused to answer his phone calls. Then, he had a man who worked for him call Beulah and tell her that Heth was a good man and that he loved her. She only replied, "I hear what you are saying". Finally, Heth got on the phone. She would only answer with closed statements (Yes, No, etc.).

∞

One day, when Beulah was visiting Heth, at his apartment,

he started begging her to stay there with him. It was a two hour drive to Raines. She said "why There is nothing for me to do here?". You stay gone from 6:00am until 9:00pm, and then you come home and stay on the computer until 1:00am. I can't swim alone, and there is no one to swim with me." A few weeks later, she figured out what was going on. He can never discuss anything. While driving home from church, on Sunday morning, she kept picking him and asked if he was going to work off shore. He said "yes". He had not asked her what she thought about it, or even mentioned it to her. He was packed and was leaving that day. Later on numerous occasions, he begged her to go with him off shore, but she refused. She finally told him to stop asking her, because she was not going. He worked off shore in El Harkins, SA and Angees, SA. For eight years. Several times he traveled to Mexico, and twice to Costa Rica.

Having been a praying person, all her life, she prayed a lot. Through these kind of trials, she grew spiritually by depending more and more on God, praying in Jesus' name, and reading the scriptures. She could not ask the church or others to pray for him, without divulging his mental condition. God showed her progressively how she had to be the strong one, and make decisions, when he could not. Family members all began to notice that he seemed strange. Beulah felt confirmed that he was Obsessive Compulsive, a Hoarder, and Melancholic.

Once when he was off shore, Heth purchased condoms, and they do not need condoms, because She had a Hysterectomy. One Condom was missing from the four pack. She told him she was sure he took it out and tried it on, because she knew he was not capable of having sex. He just wanted to make her think he was, like he thought she might be jealous. He over estimated himself.

∞

In 2000, they purchased a three bedroom Condo, on the beach, in Alabama. It sleeps ten. It has an open living room, and kitchen, a long hall, a foyer from the front entrance, and two bathrooms. The kitchen has a bar and four stools.

The weather in Alabama ranges from high 97 – 55 and low 24 – 13 degrees. As one might expect, the Gulf Coast is a few degrees hotter, than the mid or upper state. Also, the weather there is a few degrees warmer than Georgia or South Carolina.

Frank he had a double standard, one for himself and one for everyone else. Although he only went through the eighth grade, he was able to accomplish a lot. He attended school in South Carolina and Georgia, and worked on his dad's farms while growing up. He served on the board of Trustees, at the Baptist Church for years. He accepted Jesus at the age of twelve, under the Old Arbor, and was baptized that same year. He was ordained as a Deacon and served on three different building committees.

He served as active Secretary and Treasurer of the Cemetery Committee, for over twenty years. He was appointed Lieutenant Colonel Aide DeCamp, Governor's Staff, in Atlanta, Georgia. He served on the Federal Housing Administration, the Local County Welfare Board, and as a Community Committeeman on the Farm Program. He sold cemetery lots for two years in South Carolina. He was a used car dealer, both wholesale and retail for seven years. He drove a truck for a Wholesale Grocery Dealer, in his younger years, and worked in the Cotton Mill. He was never arrested, had never been in court except to serve as a Juror, serve on the Grand Jury, or as a Witness. He said that his hobby and greatest joy was studying the Holy Bible.

Before her father died, in 2001 during the Christmas Holidays they were visiting her dad. While the two of them were alone, he told her that "he tried to raise all of his children to be perfect, but she was the only "perfect" child he had. She responded "well,

I appreciate you telling me that daddy. That is so sweet of you to share that with me".

He also said, "I think Todd hates me." She said "Oh Daddy, you are so wrong." He asked what makes you think that? She replied, because a few years back, when you were both not getting alone too well, they considered selling their house and moving to town, on two occasions." However, Todd said "I just can't do it. I love daddy too much and I love this place too much." Within a week, Frank got on the phone and ordered over $50,000.00 worth of farm equipment and had it standing in Todd's yard. It was a big Tractor, hay bailer, mower, and only God knows what else.

A few years earlier, Todd was helping Frank install a new bathroom, in the home place. Frank kept yelling and screaming at Todd, unmercifully. Over the weekend, Beulah told Todd "next time he screams at you like that, you tell him, that "you do not have to let anyone talk to you like that. Calmly lay your hammer down and walk out." He did and Frank had to go hire a neighbor to help finish the bathroom.

CHAPTER EIGHT

CHOOSE LIFE OR DEATH

James 1:12 Blessed is the man that resistant temptation. KJV

During the time they were renovating the house, one of her construction workers stole Beulah's Social Security Card, and Belk Card, out of her purse, for his wife, and Beulah had to order a new one. She learned later that he had been in prison earlier. She never pressed charges.

Soon after that when she paid her employees, one week end she forgot to sign one of their checks. The bank called her and said that he had signed one of her checks. She apologized and told them that it was her fault, because they were talking when she wrote the check, and she just forgot to sign it. She told them to tell him she would come down immediately and get cash, and take it to him at his home, which is what she did. She refused to bring charges against him. She told them that he was a skilled worker and a hard working employee, and she refused to charge him with forgery.

Frank was a brilliant man. It would have been interesting to know what his IQ was. He was cruel to Todd, working him like a slave and talking to him as if he were a "dog". He promised Todd all of his life, that if he stuck with Frank and helped him work, he would inherit all the farm equipment and cattle. They farmed on halves. However, when Frank died, he willed to Todd one-third of the cattle and equipment, to Farris one-third, and to Beulah one-third. So when Celia (Executor of the will and Farris' daughter) read the will, Beulah told her that she wanted her third of cattle and equipment to go to Todd. Farris said "oh, that means that I get two-thirds." Beulah said "no, it means that Todd gets two-thirds, and you get one-third". It took weeks to get that straightened out, when they started selling off cattle and equipment. Years later, Todd told Beulah how he watched Farris' daughter and her husband load up and pull off the newest and most expensive piece of equipment, without a word to anyone about it. He had personally paid for all of it. Frank had also willed to each of his children $10,000.00. When Beulah received hers, she gave it to Todd, because she felt that he deserved it and that Frank had not treated him fairly.

Frank told her how he use to ride his bike across the road, to Todd's house, when he knew they would be eating. He would stand outside their kitchen window and listen to their conversations. He was so controlling.

Frank had a stroke fifteen or more years before he died. When her father died at age 88, she inherited the home place, where she and her siblings had grown up, and sixteen farm acres, with all the shelters, barns, cattle and equipment. They remodeled the house and all the buildings on the farm. The house was three rooms, a living room, kitchen, and bedroom. If you can imagine eight people living there, it was both parents, four girls, and two boys. It had originally been just two rooms, before Frank built the kitchen on back of the living room. The inside walls were "Tongue and Grove", which remain today (2016).

Heth kept wanting to move the house back from the road, to a hill in back, facing the lake. She would not have that. So, he insisted on building a new modern house on the hill in back. She told him "you go right ahead and build a new house. I will be living up there in those three rooms." Therefore, he said "well, we will have to add on to it." The inside wall in the living room was leaning out at the top. She had a skilled construction worker straighten it. Frank had told her before he died, not to ever try to renovate that house, because it was too old. They started renovating and tearing down shelters while they were still living in Mississippi. He kept working off shore until 2003. There were a lot of trips back and forth from Mississippi to Georgia, where she stayed some of the time. He worked two or three weeks off shore, then was home one or two weeks.

Truth is, while they were living in Raines, MS. after she had made up her mind to move back home, to Georgia, she told him that she had decided to move and that he could go find him a house wherever he wanted to live. He just ignored that. She has never asked, or suggested that he move with her, to her home place in Georgia. She considers him her "Star Boarder." They put the money from the sale of their Mississippi house in Raines, on the Condo, in Alabama, to pay off the loan.

They tore down the chicken house, double garage, wood shelter, and well house. They moved and rebuilt each of those further from the house, tore off the porches of the house, the roof, all the outside, just leaving the inside of the three rooms. They tore out two old fire places that were beyond rebuilding. The house was already over two hundred years old, then.

They built a second barn, just to house Heth's junk. Later he wanted to build a huge metal shelter, like his buddies, but she refused to let him. She finally let him build a smaller barn to work, sort and weigh Pecans for sale. Later she let him build a metal shelter half the size that he really wanted, to park the camper.

∞

In 2002, they moved from Mississippi to Georgia, in their newly renovated house. They had built two bathrooms on each end of the wrap around back porch (which they had torn out), with a wash room in between. There was now a master bedroom, and third bedroom, and a large office, with a Cathedral Ceiling. Three years later they built a carport on the east corner of the front porch. Four years later they built a large music room on the back, and a large fireplace made with "Mica" rocks, which had specks of gold in them. Frank had made the children pick up the rocks out of the back field when he cleared new ground. The remaining rock pile is still there, today. They have enjoyed years of jamming with musicians there, since.

The weather there is a few degrees cooler, year round, than in Alabama and Mississippi.

Beulah became pianist, organist and taught Sunday School at a nearby Church of God, for two years. She preached on two occasions, and their son Moses, from Tennessee preached there twice when he was visiting them. While there the pastor refused to preach on "Hell", because he said the people did not want to hear it. Therefore, Beulah predicted that something would happen to him. Then, to top that, his wife presented a Christmas program, dressed as a vagrant, and imitated a mentally retarded person. It provoked Beulah so much, that she thought about getting up and walking out, but she was scheduled next, on the program, to do music. Approximately three weeks later, she wrote a newspaper editorial citing some pastors in the area for their short comings (but, not mentioning their names). The church let this pastor and his wife go, after eighteen years of pastoring there. After that, Beulah became Pianist and Organist at a Pentecostal Holiness Church for one year.

She and Heth were spending a week at their Condo, in Alabama. She got sick and had a terrible day traveling to Raines, Mississippi, the next day. When they arrived there, she went directly to the emergency room. From there they went to visit their son Daniel and his family. The doctor put her on medication and told her to go to bed. The diagnosis was "Food Poisoning. They had gone to a Luncheon at the Condo the day before. It was a big "to do." That is where they suspected she got the bad food.

Beulah had numerous skin cancers and precancers removed from her face, neck and arms, in 2002. She had Osteoarthritis, with lots of pain all over her body and numbness in her arms and legs. She was on numerous medicines. During that year, she had three surgeries to remove a Cyst, on her left foot in the same place, on the side near her big toe. Last time the doctor had left a string in it and it got infected. After she had the skin doctor remove it, she told the surgeon about it and he was extremely sorrowful.

∞

They started visiting an elderly lady, and her daughter, who were distant relatives and good friends, in 2003. They owned a chicken farm. Beulah and Heth were fascinated with the chickens, and soon started their own chicken farming. Heth, as his usual self, became totally obsessed. He started building chicken coops, more and more against Beulah's will. He would beg to start building another one, and explain to her where and how he would build it. When she went to see it, it was nothing like what he had asked to build.

Heth was diagnosed with Precancerous Prostate. It was very upsetting to him. He had to have a couple of Biopsies, and medications to get it under control, so that he would not need to have surgery.

Beulah and Heth began taking bookings to do Music: Gospel, Bluegrass, and Country. Those included singing, of course. Some included the "Shiloam Trio." They purchased more Guitars, Banjos, a Fiddle and Cello for her. They were frequently buying updated equipment and musical instruments, and sheet music, as well as printing out music on the Computer. They made Cassettes and CD's for sale. However, they gave away more than half of them to friends and relatives.

They bought a new, modern pull camper, in 2005. Heth and Beulah camped several times a year in Federal and State Parks in Georgia, South Carolina, and North Carolina. Participating in Bluegrass Festivals and playing Music with them.

They became members of a hunting club. They had their own camper. It was primitive camping. No electricity or water. They had a dug outhouse, named after his brother's wife, and they carried their own water, and groceries. There were no shopping stores in the area – just pine trees. They had bond fires at night and played their musical instruments. They called that "Jamming. Heth's married brother had a woman hidden in his tent. Everyone could smell her perfume on him. This was while he was married to his third wife.

Once they went camping, with a group of relatives, in South Carolina. It was a good hour's drive to the camp. Before they left, Beulah asked Heth if he had packed the box of groceries, which was setting on the kitchen cabinet. He assured her that he had. When they set up camp, there were no groceries. He had to drive back home to get them. He returned with the groceries plus a cooler which she had placed on the front porch for her sister to put their mail in each day, while they were gone. He has a problem doing anything correctly.

She and Millie were walking in the pasture, one beautiful afternoon, looking over the land which they had inherited. Millie said "what is your is mine, and what is mine is yours." Beulah said very sternly "NO MAM. What is mine is not yours, and I do not want what is yours.."

She was picking up limbs under a Pecan Tree, on a Cloudy morning, and stumbled backwards over a large limb. Not long after that, she was chasing after her little Chihuahua, who was running toward the road, and she fell flat of her belly. It knocked the breath out of her. A few weeks after that, she was washing kitchen cutlery and the electric knife slipped and cut the back of her right index finger, almost to the bone. She grabbed a pint jar half full of Kerosene, which had probably set down in the cabinet for fifty years (It had turned dark rust color), poured over it, and called her husband to take her to the emergency room. The doctor said it needed stitches, but was afraid to use Novocain or anything to numb her finger, because of her allergies. Therefore, she insisted that he do it without any medication, which he did. It took two stitches, in the back of her finger nail, which over time, gradually flattened her nail, a little bit. In the past, she had dental work without anything to deaden or numb it, on several occasions. Some dentist refuse to do dental work on someone who has Mitral Valve problems. She had studied about people, who feel rejected, are more inclined to have accidents, and she believed it.

Beulah insisted that Heth take her to see her first home, and the Mill Hill, in South Carolina, in 2002. She remembered eighteen steps from the back porch, but there was only six. While Heth made pictures of the house, and referred to it as her home, she felt validated for the first time. She recalled that little girl who sat there in that chair and belonged to people who loved her. Her parents never once mentioned it. No one ever talked about she lived with her maternal grandparents, and she blocked it out of her mind, until she was in her thirties. She began having nightmares and seeing her grandpa Woodall. From that time on she began remembering things. After her parents died she began talking about it to her relatives. Her siblings thought that she was crazy, and said that she was lying. However, when her aunts and uncles communicated with her, remembering things they did together with her, more and more her siblings began to believe her.

∞

Heth retired in 2003. He was so cruel to Beulah, that her health began to fail. All he had ever done was work; think about his career and getting rich, sports, and fame. Her medical doctor and surgeon tried to get her to find another man. She told them that she had made up her mind that she would not do that to her children, that she would just endure and when she dies she will go to heaven. She kept telling Heth that she just wanted peace. She kept begging God to restore her peace and joy in Jesus Christ. It got to where she could not even pray or read her bible. She was use to living alone, while he was gone off shore, two or three weeks at a time. He came home for two weeks, then was gone, again.

They were married fifty years, before he ever called her by her name. After moving back home, near relatives, he started calling her by her name. He just always said what he had to say. He still rarely calls her by her name and only around others. He never bought her flowers of gifts of any kind, and was above saying "please" or "thank you." He lied habitually. Sometimes, he would say "I know that you are smarter than me," then act like he was pouting. She always tried to help him, and would never take advantage of him. He seemed to hate her all the time. He argued and was negative about everything. Her chest felt like it was full of brick, most of the time. It hurt all the time. She could hardly get her breath, every day. She prayed and begged God, all the time, to restore, to her, the peace, and joy of Jesus Christ. It was only by the grace of God that she survived each day. Heth has always read at the table. If nothing else, he would read labels on cereal boxes or jars. He sits on the commode, roosts, and reads. Beulah had to cancel the daily newspaper, because he would read every word in it and procrastinate. Letting work pile up or letting her do the work. He cannot communicate in the mornings, until after he eats. His brain is so slow, that he cannot comprehend. Part of his problem is that he cannot hear good, especially while he is chewing, and many times he does not have his hearing aids on. He is such an Introvert.

After he retired, he became more obsessive/compulsive and more of a hoarder.

She has learned that she would rather be poor and experience the peace and joy of the Lord, than to be rich and live with a maniac, a scrooge, a miser, or someone who worships riches, and loves money. She knows God (John 17:3 KJV) and can discern spirits. Work ethics was introduced to her at age seven. She became her dad's work hand, and her mama's maid. They treated her like a slave. They showed her no affection. They had abandoned her to her Maternal Grandparents, until she was age five. Because she was smart and intelligent, they and her husband took advantage of her, and used her every way they could find, while all the time putting her down and intimidating her. She has the gift of giving, and caring for others. She obeyed God, and her parents. Her favorite two songs are "I'd Rather Have Jesus," and "He is So Precious To Me." When she married she told Heth those are the two songs, which she wants sung at her funeral. He made a note and put it into his billfold. He still carries that.

One morning at 5:30am Heth told Beulah that her going to church and religion "was all in her head." That was one of his major responses to a lot of circumstances, to defend himself.

In 1998 he started "Heth Ross Apparel Consultant, LLC, and put it in her name, because the government would not charge him taxes. Many men took advantage of the ruling and put businesses in their wife's name.

All those dreams of having a beautiful retirement, of living together after retirement became a huge joke. It was a hell. He would twist words, argue and fuss all the time. He was negative about everything and impossible to get alone with. She could not communicate with him. Her MD, Chiropractor, and Surgeon all tried to get her to leave him.

In the past, they had cats and dogs, at least one or both at a time. They bought food, gave them their shots, and flea treatment, etc. And, never had a problem with any of that. After he retired, he refused to let Beulah have a pet. He said they were too expensive, and too much trouble.

∞

Farris repeatedly told Beulah, that she was planning to fertilize two Crepe Myrtle trees, in a row of seven, in the Church yard across the road. She said they were not growing as fast, nor blooming as pretty as the others. Beulah kept telling her not to do it, that she might kill them, because it was too hot. She finally did it late one evening after dark. She came and told Beulah next day. Beulah was frantic. She went up that evening to see what Farris had done. She prayed frequently, that those trees would not die. They lived.

Farris had already cut down a Red Bud tree, while they were out of town. Beulah had told her repeatedly, that she could not cut it down. It was one Heth had moved there, from another state, when they moved. When Beulah returned, Farris asked "do you see anything different, since you have been gone?" She said, "you did not cut down our Red Bud tree?" She said "yes I think the yard looks better." Tears came into Beulah's eyes, but she would not let Farris see them. Later she started talking about fertilizing a Lilac bush, that had been almost dormant for years. It was one that Beulah and Cassie had set out, when Beulah was a child. Farris did it, while she was out of town, and it died.

Beulah had a Colonoscopy in 2003. The doctor removed a cluster of six tumors from her Anus, which were precancerous. The doctor said on a scale of 1 -10 they were an 8. He also removed a polymp.

∞

In 2004, as they were leaving the Condo, he let her out of the car, to go in WalMart and buy her some pain medicine. When she came out he was not there. She panicked and was ready to call the Police, when she saw him parked way down at the far corner of the parking lot, with the driver door open, and his legs sticking out, listening to music, on the car radio. It was very hot and he had moved the car down to a shade. She thought he had left her on purpose, because he had done such a thing before.

One night they were waiting up late for Moses and his family to arrive, from Tennessee, for a three day visit. It is a ten hour drive from their house. They had not seen them for six months. Heth had packed up his clothes in a suitcase to sleep in another room, to make room for their guest. He put his clothes in the car and left. She knew he was going to do that. He was so missing his travels abroad, his work, and staying in motels. She did not know where he went. She called his mother next day. She did not know. Next he showed up at her house at the same time Moses and his family were visiting her. They all came home and he said to Beulah that he "just came to stay a little while. "But, later he asked if he could stay. She said "no one told you to leave, to start with," Weeks later when the credit card bill came, she was checking off charges, and asked him what a charge was for on the motel bill. He wrote in red, "the day I ran away."

A few weeks later, Heth gave a testimony that sounded like a synopsis of a fiction novel. He told things that were not true and she had never heard of before. He told it so sweetly and convincingly.

Heth had surgery for another Hernia. It was across the front of his abdomen. Again, they inserted a mesh. While the hospital was releasing him, he insisted that he was going to drive home. He refused to listen to Beulah about letting her drive. She had to get his pastor to talk with him, to let her drive home.

During June and July of 2007, Beulah was seeing four doctors: MD, Chiropractor, Arthritis Specialist, and Surgeon. He did surgery on her left shoulder. She had testing done and found out that she was seriously allergic to everything she breathed. Doctors put her on allergy shots which she took once a week, for a year. They told her that she would need to take them four more years. She said "I don't think so." She lost her voice for six months due to Acid Reflux and could not speak or sing. She had to take voice therapy to learn how to talk again. She had to have a stress test, and Hide-a-Scan, and was allergic to the Dye. She went blind for half of the day,. She lay in the Emergency Room for three hours. They did a CT on her head and found no problem. After the vision gradually started coming back, they dismissed her.

Beulah began typing her second book in 2006. That same year Beulah fell off the back of the Gator (four wheeler) while it was moving, in a hay field. The ambulance picked her up and took her to the emergency room. They X-rayed her neck, twice, then called her in to look at the results, on the screen. One half of her third neck vertebrae was missing. The doctor said it was not fresh blood and determined that it must have happened in a 1953 auto accident which doctors called a "Whiplash."

Around 2008, they were musicians in a Pentecostal Holiness Church. He was Guitarist and she was Pianist/Organist. They always practiced the day before they had a performance anywhere, or on Sunday for Church services. He would insist that she sing and play with him over each verse, until he found the perfect key for him to play and sing in. He cannot read music, and cannot keep correct time on any song. He just plays his own thing. She would do however he wanted by following him. He would get up in church and start to play, then turn to her and say, "you are in the wrong key." She would say "I am in the key which you marked it." She got tired of being humiliated and doing everything his way. Therefore, she accepted a paid position as Organist/Pianist at a Baptist Church, and he followed. She held that position for three and a half years.

Beulah habitually talked to the pastor after church about he was preaching "Humanism", and not preaching the full Gospel. He was not preaching about the gifts of the spirit, about the Holy Spirit, or about Hell. He resented her comments, and said the church told him not to preach on those things, before they hired him. After two years there, the Pastor announced that he was planning to change the church, but he was not ready to tell what he was going to do. Later in his message he said that he was planning to start a prayer chain. He pointed his finger at Beulah, called her name and said that he was planning to talk with her. After he asked her to lead this prayer group, she declined saying that she was already praying for the church and others who had already left the church. He began to put her down, and started accusing her of not letting her husband be head of the household.

He began to build her husband up. He hid the Organ plug-in, so that she could not play the organ.

Months later, he came out to her house and said that a few years back God had told him that He was sending him a Prophetess to help him in the church, and he believed she was that person. He said that the Baptist Conference was going under (not his words but her's – paraphrased), and he wanted her to help him change the church over to "Full Gospel." She refused and proceeded to tell him what she thought about him. She told him why Heth cannot be head of his household. That being: his mother was boss of his family, since his dad was an alcoholic and stayed gone a lot. He was never taught to do anything, except help farm. He was incapable of managing anything. He sits around plays his guitar, sings, or listens to music, on the computer, with his ear buds on. She has to treat him like her little boy. Her second son told her "Well, mother you can't help it that you are smart." Brilliant boy!!

When/if Heth works outside, he has to have the radio on, with his ear buds in. He also, sits for hours and sews by hand, mending and patching his socks, under shorts, and "T" shirts. They have patches on patches. He wears them after they are shreds. He has drawers of new underclothes, "T" shirts, and socks that he has never worn. He will wear the nicer, old ones to church, etc.

Beulah has the gift of "giving". Her vision is to do God's will, and her desire is to be like Jesus, and serve others. Her desire is not so much to preach or minister in music to large crowds, or become famous. She wants her life to count for Jesus, endlessly. She aims to remain pliable, that God can have His way with her, and to be Altruistic. She just wants to please and obey God. She wants to experience the joy and peace daily, which Jesus gives. On her tombstone, she wants engraved "Here lays a woman who is rich toward God." Heth will always be a pauper. He will always have a "poor boy" mentality.

Their second granddaughter got married in 2009.

Next morning she told Heth that she was going to hire someone to haul off the scrap lumber and the pile of brush limbs which he had not burned for over a year. As well as hire someone to get the leaves off the yard. He blew up and said if she hired someone, he would throw all of her things/belongings out of the house. Now, she owns the house and farm. She inherited it from her dad seven years ago. Heth has been the star boarder. She never told or asked him to move there with her. He kept saying he was going to build her a new house on the back hill. She told him that she was going to live in that three room house. Therefore, he said well, we will build onto it. Remember back in the 1960's he said that if she tried to divorce him, he would kill her. She is a possessed commodity. He was building his ninth chicken house against her will. He begged permission to build the last one. He showed and explained where and how it would be. Later before he finished it, she went down to see what he was doing. He had built it much larger, inside one of the vehicle shelters, and for a different purpose than he had said.

∞

March of 2009, they bought three Time Share Condos, in Tennessee. Beulah received her Doctorate Degree in Theology, from Evans First, in Lark Alabama. Heth started gardening and they canned and froze delicious vegetables, and fruit from the Farm They have a Pecan Orchard, and sell Pecans. Also, they pick out Pecans and freeze them. Later they thaw and roast what is left.

Heth's mother died in 2009. That same year, Saul (Beulah's oldest brother) died. This was a tough year. The market fell.

First week in January, 2009, Heth's financial statements began coming in for 2008 showing significant losses, totaling up to half a million dollars. He worried about not having enough money to last until they died, not to mention all the phone calls and e-mails he made to their sons about the same subject. Also, he kept calling Realtors who rent their Condo, in Alabama, three times a week for three weeks. He tried to commit suicide, on January the eighteenth. They came home from church that evening, sat down to eat, and he started talking about finances. Again, she noticed that he was white as a sheet. He began saying that she wrote a check, for over 2K, which she did not write and she told him to apologize. He said 'I will not apologize for something I did not do. I will kill myself. When he said that, he jumped up, ran to the door, and grabbed the gun (which was standing beside the door), ran outside, toward the barns and field, and she lost sight of him. It was getting dark. Beulah was screaming repeatedly "don't do this, come back". She had not noticed the gun. He usually kept all his guns in a safe place together. For a few minutes, she was in shock and just walked the floor. As much as she wanted to live without him, she could not let him kill himself, mostly because of their children and grand children, who adored him. So, she called 911. Within fifteen minutes, the sheriff, police, EMC, and dogs were all over the place. They found him after about half an hour, sitting on a terrace, in the middle of the field, with his gun. He fought them. He was delirious, and hallucinating. They told him that if he did not stop fighting them, and refusing to let them take his guns, and he had to sign an agreement or they were taking him to jail. He finally agreed to let a friend take the guns home with him and agreed to only let them take him to the hospital. Looking back, she realized that he had been planning this. The preacher tried to shake hands with him at church and Heth looked like he was in another world. He was white as a sheet. Of course, he blamed Beulah. In the hospital he told doctors that he was upset, because Beulah wrote a check for over $2,000.00, which was a lie. Later that night they released him to his younger brother, and Beulah did not know where he was. She had not gone to the hospital, because she was afraid of him. While at his brother's, he told his pastor not to tell her where he was. She told him that his sons wanted to know where he was. When she guessed where he was the pastor agreed.

After three days, his brother brought him home. He was still white as a sheet. He walked in the door and said "I can leave or I can stay." Beulah said "no one told you to leave to start with." Things were very quiet from that day on. He was a totally different man. He was humble, tried to be truthful, refused to argue or fuss and really tried to be positive. He was agreeable most of the time, with few exceptions. He was good after his suicide attempt. Yeah? That only lasted about three weeks. She never felt loved by him, after the first two years they were married, when he decided to have a career. He quit showing any affection. Everything was just about career and money.

From that time Heth decided to have a career, he was like a runaway train that kept gaining momentum, until it finally wrecked in January 2009, with attempted suicide. Her hatred for his behavior overshadowed her love for him. that too was a progression. After he retired she despised him and could not tolerate being around him.

Months later she, figured out what he was blaming her for. He had set her up months earlier. When the Financial Institution Agent had recently stopped by, they each bought another annuity. Hers was $2,200.00. She immediately went and pulled her file, and check book to pay for her's. He started to insist that she write it from their joint checking account, which was so out of character for him. She had not written any checks from the joint account to any of her accounts. He was so sweet about it, and the agent was sitting there witnessing all of it. Beulah honestly thought that he was changing, from his old stingy self. For about two years he would threaten to kill himself, when he got frustrated.

When she gets into difficult situations, she takes a minute and asks herself "what would Jesus do if he were in this kind of situation." Since that event, she has learned to tell Heth what to do, and take the initiative to get things done. She learned years ago, that she must do what God wants first, and secondly what her husband wants, only if it is in God's will. She does not live under the curse of Adam. She is a daughter of God's and lives in the liberty of Christ.

Heth has never learned how to use a cell phone. He has had three. He will not be a part of her phone program, but buys minutes which he rarely uses. He transfers them each year. When she calls him, he does not answer. After he gets home and she tells him that she called, he says, "Oh, I heard it ring and vibrate, but I did not know if anyone was calling." If she needs a ride home, or any emergency, it is still the same. She has to call relatives or friends, if she needs help. She is allergic to almost everything she eats, and lots of medications.

Early one morning, he had threatened her, because she told him she was going to hire someone to clean the yard. Two days before, he had thrown things in the kitchen, when she suggested that he soap up his hands to wash, before drying on the towel. He has his own bathroom, but comes into the kitchen to wash his hands, but only wets his fingers and dries on the towel (wets and wipes). This has been going on for seven years. He refuses to be agreeable. Therefore, she had Diarrhea for a long, long time. Finally, she went to a Gastrologist. When he diagnosed her with a Bacterial infection, which was caused from Feces, he said it is usually caught from a family member. She told him about Heth refused to use any kind of soap or antibacterial liquid. The doctor agreed that Heth had Bacterial Disease. However, he did not have any symptoms. They had to take Antibiotic medicines for three months.

His dad was an alcoholic, and did not stay home regularly. He would leave for several weeks at a time. Back then, his mother made her brush brooms and kept the yard swept clean. People did not cut their lawns. They dug and cut out grass, to maintain their yard. Heth never learned to do any yard work. He thought the wife was supposed to do all of that. He will not do it, and will not let her hire anyone to do it. So, she has to do it, or it does not get done. This has been a great issue, because she is no longer able to do most of it anymore.

They traveled to their condo, on the Gulf Coast, Alabama. They go down there twice a year, because they have it listed as "Rental Property". The IRS only allows them to stay in it two weeks a year, with exceptions for cleaning or repairs, etc. They spent the first night in a resort, in Birmingham,. Alabama. Next morning, they started out with no snow, but it gradually started snowing. They drove on the interstate, in a snow storm, for three hours. Large flakes were coming down heavily. The snow got so high between 3" – 6". It was a pure "wonderland." They were talking about stopping and finding a lodge. Soon there came trucks putting out salt on the bridge and highway, which they followed. They had not seen another vehicle. Things started getting better and the snow let up. What was on the highway began to melt. After about an hour, it turned into rain. They drove in rain for another hour, before reaching their destination. During the whole trip, it was very windy, making it even more difficult to travel.

Arriving, the sky was grey and the ocean was dark Thalo Blue/Black (not quite Paynes Gray Black). In the Condo, for three days and nights, the wind howled and whistled causing flopping, banging, and knocking noises. She had eaten too much and too many things which she was allergic to. Her insides were sore and hurting from her throat to her anus. She felt nauseated, had acid reflux, and diarrhea, for three days and nights.

They found a Church of God, to attend, on Sunday morning only a few miles from the Condo. It was very large, lights were turned down very low (they could not read the songs), and had contemporary, loud music, which they could hardly tolerate. The pastor tried to make everything humorous, (silly/sic) and the speaker admittedly was not a minister. He was hardly familiar with the scriptures. She could have preached a much more spirit filled sermon. When they left, she felt like she had been in a Baptist Church. It was such a disappointing event for her. After church they, stuffed themselves, again, at a Fish Camp. Then, they shopped for supplies to repair, and replace things at the Condo, which is rental property.

Heth worked every day, painting, and touching up spots on walls and chairs. He sanded the patio, Cyprus table and chairs, and repaired kitchen bar stools. He shampooed the living room carpet, replaced chairs in two bedrooms (one each) called maintenance to restore phone services and net work service, and the remote control. They had to replace a coffee maker, can opener, a set of cookware and a set of dishes. People steal things and some things wear out, or get broken. They cleaned out the inside storage room, and carried some of the stuff to the outside storage room, on the patio. All of her books and magazines were gone. Guest and friends will rent two suites next to each other, swap dishes, pans, etc, and never return them.

Just riding makes Beulah sore (she has Osteoarthritis and Pseudo Gout). On Tuesday they went to a nearby shopping mall. They had stopped and walked around in several clothes and shoe stores. She went to the restroom and when she got up off the stool, she had a catch in the bend of her back and could hardly stand. She had a difficult time walking to the car. When she got there, from then on, she had to use her walking stick (which she kept in the car), which she had not needed for eight months, or longer.

They left the mall shopping center to return to the condo, not knowing that people were celebrating the Mardi Gras (Fat Tuesday). They got into a traffic jam about 2:30pm, and another parade about 3:30pm. It took an hour to go five miles. She was in gross pain with her back, hips, and eyes and needed desperately to get to the condo, to get her medicines. After fussing until it was embarrassing, she finally laid back in her seat, closed her eyes, and practiced silence.

The trip back home takes two days one way. By the time they reached their destination, her eyes felt raw. She had cataract surgery one month prior, on her left eye and could not wear her trifocals, because she had not had the surgery on the right eye. They had to go to the pharmacy and buy ointment for her left eye, to read with used dollar store magnifying glasses. For distance, she wore her trifocals, with a patch on the left eye. The irritation is caused by wind, sun, air conditioner, or heat blowing in the vehicle.

In the north mountains, because there was a lack of rode signs. They needed to go south, but were traveling north. Neither of them thought to look at the compass to see which way they were going. They had to ask where they were, when they stopped to eat, which did not help much. They drove forty miles (one way) out of the way, and by this time it was dark. He decided to stop and visit his brother, in route home. They left there around 10:00pm, getting home after midnight. They had driven for ten hours straight. About 3:00am she woke up with such pain in her right back and chest, she could not move. They called the ambulance, which took her to the emergency room, gave her some medicine to relax her, and sent her home. It was a "Gallbladder attack." Traveling is for the birds, she says, and having rental property is a fantasy.

Here it is and they have not attempted to make love or have sex in six years. They slept together, occasionally, when they had overnight guest, or camp. During those few times, they might have hugged one or two times, within a week. Heth's career dominated and controlled their lives. She had an identity crises in1964, and in 2003 when he retired, a total of eighteen years.

She found her missing, wooden, cooking spoon under his bed mattress, at the head of the bed. He could not/would not explain it, when she confronted him. He said that he had no idea what it was doing there. No one had slept in this house or been in his bedroom, except him and her. She has her own opinion of why it was there.

He could not have a close relationship with anyone. He has problems in relationships, morality, religion, and boundaries. He grew up just doing whatever he pleased. His mother was the boss. She could not keep up with him. She said that after school, he would go down to the woods and stay until dark. He would tell her that he was looking for firewood, but did not bring in any. Heth will lie to anyone about anything. He will try to cheat anyone. He does not know a lie from the truth.

Beulah learned shortly after she was married that if you have "this", you don't have "that," and if you have "that," you don't have "this" (whatever it is).

It is said that everyone is dying from the minute they are born. It is something most people don't think about, to EXPECT to die from the minute you are born.

CHAPTER NINE

HELL ON EARTH

Psalm 103:2 Bless the Lord...who forgives all thine
iniquities: who healeth all thy diseases. KJV

During the cold winter months, of 2005, Beulah started having Diarrhea and Gastritis. It continued to grow worse, in spite of her diet changes and medications. After months, she finally went to a Gastrologist.

In January 2011, Beulah finished her first book, and had it printed.

In March 2012, they came back from Markus Island, Georgia. Heth unloaded the vehicle, and threw grocery bags, and packages under his office work table. A week or two later, when Beulah tried to get him to sort them out and put them where they belonged, he threw a temper tantrum and said he was going to throw away all her things.

Their oldest granddaughter was married June of 2001.

Heth had spells of threatening to commit suicide, since the first time he tried it in January of 2009. This morning he threatened it, again. He could not remember how to adjust the flapper of the Commode water basin, so that it would flush without holding the handle down, or hesitating. He said "I can just get my gun and shoot myself". That was after she had said she would get someone else to do it. She said "that is sic thinking". He then fixed it and said "if that don't work, you can just call a plumber". She said "I will do that". Then he pouted and would not speak for the rest of the day. By now, her greatest concern was not that he might kill himself. It was that he might kill her, or both of them.

Having been a praying person, all her life, she prayed a lot. Through these kinds of trials, she grew spiritually by depending more and more on God, praying in Jesus' name, and reading the scriptures. She could not ask the church or others to pray for him, without divulging his mental condition. God showed her progressively how she had to be the strong one.

Their son Moses called, sounding panicky, about sundown, from his home in TN. Heth had made reservations for Moses, on their Condo points, so that it cost Moses nothing to stay in their condo, and work, in that area, for a week. Heth had to cancel the reservations, which he had, made in Moses' name. Later Moses' wife told them that his "hard drive had crashed", and that he had to be on Conference calls all day. Therefore, the P.C. repair man had been there all day. Moses owns a Research Business and does most of his work by phone, in his office, at home. He has numerous employees.

Knowing that she had a worn out right hip and knee, and had obtained a power chair, five walking canes, and two walkers, just in the last year, and not to mention that she has to take medicine for her lungs and heart. She has Cardiac Disease: Mitral Valve Regurgitation and Aorta Regurgitation. She tried to get him on the Walky-Talky, but he has the radio ear plugs in his ears and one of his hearing aids is broken.

When he turned around, he moved the radio ear plugs and she started telling him that he was "ABSOLUTELY STUPID". Anyone who would put a Walky-Talkie in his pocket, then put ear plugs in his ears is "STUPID." He remained totally calm, with the attitude that she was the one who was crazy. He always tells her that "it is all in her mind," when he does something wrong. She has, on several occasions, cried and kindly, sadly begged him to please not talk to her so hatefully.

He just ignores her. When he came to the house, Beulah told him again how "STUPID" he was. She thought about using the cell phone, but he doesn't carry it with him, except on long trips. Even then, he does not know how to answer it, or send messages/calls. He refuses to use the walkie-talkies, or cell phone, as a means of communicating. He had to keep his radio on, for entertainment, he said. These problems happen daily. She yelled all the way from the house, calling his name, until he turned around and saw her, just as she got up to the pasture fence, near him. He left her no option, but to walk fast AS SHE COULD DOWN ACROSS THE FIELD IN THE DARK. She was too old and worn out to run. When she fussed at him because she had to run all the way down there after him, he said, that he did not like the inconvenience of using those things, told her that it was easier for him to drive her gator and he liked to drive her Gator best. She said "WELL, it is alright to inconvenience everyone else (meaning her), but heaven forbid that anyone inconvenience "little Heth". He did not say any more. However, next day he drove his Four Wheeler to pick up Pecans.

It was February 2009, Heth was picking up Pecans in the pasture about a quarter mile from the back of the house Beulah's brother Todd had recently cut the hay and it was still laying on the ground, and hard to walk through, without snagging it on your feet. Especially, for Beulah, who has a tendency to drag her feet, and was weak form illness

She could not figure out how Heth could see to pick up Pecans in the dark. It gets dark about 5:00pm EST, but he doesn't come in until about 8:30 or 9:00pm, for supper. He wears gloves and scrapes through the Pecans feeling them along the leaves. He is an extremist and perfectionist. Things matter more to him than people. No Altruism. The devil never ceases to ruin Beulah's day, at least once, through her selfish husband. No matter how good she tried to be to him. He thinks that he and what he wants is all that matters. There were totally no social skills there. Beulah has a tendency to drag her feet, and was weak from illness, not to mention that she has to take medicines for her lungs and heart. She thought "I will get in my Gator (four wheeler), and drive down there to get Heth. However, he had taken it. He pulls a 5' metal trailer behind his Four Wheeler, and can do the same work with it as he can with her Gator. They had numerous arguments, in the past; about he will not drive his four-wheeler, except to go hunting, once or twice a year. She cannot drive the thing, because it is too rough and jerky for her even to try cranking it.

In 2010, after serving and waiting on her for two years, during her illnesses, Heth woke up on a Sunday morning, about a week before Christmas, and could not walk. He had pain down his right leg and back. He was diagnosed with a bulged disk (L-3/4), and Sciatic nerve pain. So, he took over her electric wheel chair, walker, walking sticks, etc. and she had to serve both of them as best she could. She had not driven the car in two years. So, she had to drive to church, twenty miles away. They were both musicians in the church. Then, there was the problem of finding someone to drive him to the specialist, pain doctor, one and half hours away. A friend from church volunteered several times, and Heth's sister Joy drove them several times. He had a chair lift installed on the back of the car.

He went off shore to work for a week. It took him two weeks to write reports, email and mail to eight people, when he returned. Then, the phone calls and emails increased to discuss reports. When he left the plant down there, he left all of his clothes in the manager's office, in two big boxes, and explained that he would be back in two weeks. However, when he returned the clothes were all gone, and he had to buy new clothes.

Sometimes, Beulah just wished that she could run away, somewhere and hide, from the memories of her parents and her husband. She never dreamed of being rich or having a big house. She wanted about four children, even if she lived in a log cabin, down by the river. She just wanted to experience, the joy, peace, and love of Jesus Christ. However, God has blessed her above what she could ask or think, when it comes to her children and grandchildren. Praise God!!!!!!

Beulah had Cataract Surgery on her left eye, and two weeks later on the right eye, in 2010. She went to an Arthritis Doctor, for pain in her limbs, and shoulders. He diagnosed her with Osteoarthritis, and Pseudo Gout. After several visits, he sent her to a Surgeon for a left shoulder replacement. However, the Surgeon did a Micro Scope Surgery instead. She was incapacitated for about two years.

Besides Heth's brood of thirty-five chickens, he had seven Turkeys. They started climbing up the six steps, to the porch and look in the glass of the sliding doors. Heth figured that they were looking for a mate. When they went to Garage Sales, looking for a mirror for her, he bought one and took it to a place in the Turkey yard, for them to look at themselves. She threatened to kill them, shoot them, or give them away. He would just laugh. Not to be outdone, she remembered that she had one option that he was not familiar with. She prayed that God would get rid of those Turkeys. She did not care how, or if it was all at once or one at a time. Within two days two got run over by cars, running on the road, in front of the house. Some critter got the rest of them.

They were all gone within a few days. He has not bothered to get anymore Turkeys.

It was almost sunset, in 2011, when Heth asked her to go with him to S.C. (about forth miles) to see a man (whom he met on line) about buying some chickens. He stopped to buy gas and decided to back into the very tight space for a pump. He lost his mind. He put that car in forward gear four times, and almost ran into a truck, before he finally put it into reverse. Beulah kept asking him what was wrong with him, but he did not speak a word. He kept getting lost before they found their destination. It was very dark by time they left to return home. He started driving in the opposite direction to where they needed to go. She kept trying to correct him, and begged him to let her drive, but he argued that he was correct. They drove miles out in the desolate, wooded country, before he finally relented to turn around and go the other way. She vowed that if/when she got home; she would not go anywhere again, with him.

Heth thinks that paper towels are cheaper than napkins. Therefore, he will not use napkins. He tears a paper towel in half, rolls one side up and leaves it on the table where he sits, for the next meal. He saves Banana peels, strings, and rag from every Banana he eats. He lays them around on tables, chairs, desk, or floors, or anywhere through-out all the house, before he gets them outside to his flowers, plants, etc. He has to have a Banana daily for breakfast.

This morning she was sick and not able to go to church. He went to his room and pulled out all his pants (ten or twelve pair) threw them onto the floor and said he wanted them washed. She refused to wash them. He had to wash them. Their children were coming for Christmas Holidays. She had everything to do to prepare for their visit. What triggered his rage, was that she tried to talk to him about he does not put his clothes in the washing for her to keep them clean. He just wears them over and over, until she has to tell him he smells. He mends and patched his clothes (mostly underclothes and socks), even after they become shreds. He has more clothes than he can ever wear in a life time, but he saves them. His dresser drawers, Chester draws, and boxes in the attic are full of clothes. He has had an uncle, a brother-in-law, and two friends who died and he inherited their clothes, some of which have never been worn. Also, his children have given him clothes. She quit buying him anything, years ago, because he forbids her to buy him gifts.

For several years, Heth has been haughty, arrogant, high minded, and proud. He has become a stranger, and we do not know what to expect next, from him. He who does not love does not know God, for God is love, John 3:13. During 2013 and several years previously, she and relatives of their families noticed that Heth was definitely a hoarder, and Obsessive/Compulsive, as well as Narcistic. Narcisticism was so totally out of character, for him, because he had, during his whole life shown signs of Paranoah, as well as an Introvert. He had by now shown definite signs of Dementia. He would leave water faucet's running, leave doors open, leave cabinets open, leave things set partly off the edge of the table and could not find the drinking glasses without help, which always set inside the first, top cabinet next to the sink. She asked his doctor to do some testing to determine if medication would help the type of Alzheimer's he had. His doctor had a head scan made to see if medications would help him. She said that he did not need the medication, but he was Anemic. Being a psychologist, she put him on Iron tablets and he improved tremendously.

The things that have kept her alive are: God and Jesus. She is a daughter of God's, she refuses to be negative, therefore staying positive, she refuses to eat like a pig, and she refuses to care what others, think. She prays when she wakes up in the morning, then she rebukes Satan and tells him that he "will not possess her mind today," in Jesus' name.

She got shingles 10/11, on the left of her Anus and Virgina. It started out with the flesh turning very red, sore, and painful, which lasted two days. Then, it broke out in whelps for two days. Next the whelps turned into blisters for 2 days, which burst and had scales for several days. Low and behold a few days later it broke out in whelps, again. The pain got so sever for twenty-four hours, she could not sleep or hardly do anything. That is when she called her Dermatologist. When the nurse got her seated in a room, the doctor came in smiling sweetly. Greeted her and sat down in the corner of the room. She was seated on the side of the room across from the exam table. The doctor looked real solemn at her and said "so, you have a problem below". She said "yes". He said "show me." She proceeded to tell him what happened, from the beginning to the end. He still looked at her solemnly and said "show me." She looked startled and said "you mean me turn my bottom up to your face. He said "yes". She just sat there and said "I thought you would ask me to lie on the table". At that time the nurse said "Come get on the table." The doctor said lie on your side. She said "which way". He said "it doesn't matter." With his rubber gloves on, he parted her hams, looked and said "you have Shingles." He wrote her a five day Rx, which he said might help a little. As she parted he smiled and said he hoped the Rx helped, and that she would feel better. He said he did not know how long it would take to heal. After three weeks, it was still sore whelps, and she cannot remember how long it took to finally heal.

That same Dermatologist did six surgeries on her face, for one cancer (on the forehead), two Basal Cell Carcinomas, and three tumors all on her face. Then, put her on a special cocktail of four medicines in one Hormone cream, which she had to drive twenty miles, to another city, to have replenished once a month, for a year.

Her sneezing, too loud, brought Heth's complaints. He had already calculated the volume of my sneezes, and they did not meet his expectations. When living alone, she did not have to please anyone, but God and herself. During their whole marriage, she got to eat most of her meals, alone. He could hardly ever come to a meal, on time, even if he did happen to be in the house.

Sister Drusie became disabled and had to move to Virginia to live with her son. She had to sell all of her property, which was two farms, and her car. Seven years later, her youngest sister Millie moved back into the farm, which she had inherited from her dad. She had lived in N.C. and they had not seen her for seven years.

When Beulah turned eighty years old, her children gave her a birthday party, in her church Fellowship Hall. It was a blast. They went all out and did not miss anything. It was the only birthday party she ever had. She vowed that from that day forward she was reinventing herself. Giving up was not an option. She must increase her faith, by speaking the "word", and believing deeper. Conviction, commitment, and submission, that is where it is. Jesus is the only way.

Heth went fishing in Scales, South Carolina, with his brother, his brother's wife, and his sister for five days. On the fourth day, which he was gone, Beulah discovered that she barely had running water. They were living in the country and on a well, with a pump. She went outside and found that he had left the water running where he watered his chickens. She called him on his brother's phone number, because he does not know how to answer his cell phone. He seemed unconcerned about it. So, she just made do until he got home, next day, and let him get it repaired.

Beulah cooked supper for Heth, and had it on the table. He came in, got a frozen Pot Pie out of the freezer, and ate it, and did not touch the food she prepared. He never said a word, just left the kitchen. She noticed that he was eating Pot Pies frequently, even though she had food prepared.

Beulah's twin, girls, great granddaughters were born in March of 2014, to her second granddaughter. Both have red, curled hair, and blue eyes. Both favor so most of the family still cannot tell them apart, most of the time.

In April of 2014, their son Daniel retired from thirty-three years of military duty and moved from Mississippi to Georgia. He purchased his grandfather Shiloam's home place, which also was his great grandfather's. It sat on two acres of land. Later in October he bought the balance of the farm which was eleven acres. It is next door to where his parents live. The house was built in 1889, and was a beautiful antebellum house, with a Smoke House, a double garage, twenty eight boat shelter (to rent out). He renovated the whole house (inside and out) putting on a new metal/tin roof, after removing three shingle roofs, which had just been added to what was there. He added a new bedroom making it a three bedroom, added a new large bathroom making it two bathrooms, and made a foyer into a wash room. He had the chimneys rebuilt and put expensive gas heaters in two fireplaces, and put in a new wood heater in one side of the double fireplace.

Heth made Beulah pay him for cutting grass with their tractor and doing construction work on barns. She talked with God about how she could handle that. God told her that "it is alright for her to play by his rules." Therefore, she started charging one half the cost of expenses, for him to use the camper, and traveling on vacations and trips, without her. Those which she chose to stay home. He has to have one or more trips planned ahead all the time, to look forward to. He is obsessed with staying away from home. So, he takes his siblings with him. They are all anxious to travel somewhere.

It was probably about April 2013, when she went to a "Red Hat Club" meeting. Heth was suppose to pick her up in town, when she was to come home. She called the home cell phone numbers and got "no answer". Finally she got a club member to take her home and paid her. Beulah knocked on the front and side doors and no answer. After a while, she went to the back door to the music room and he was sitting in there picking his guitar and singing with a CD playing.

Beulah is glad that she paid tuition for her children and grandchildren to go to school. She has five doctors in the family. She and Heth were the first in each of their families to go to college.

She started going to a Non-Denominational Church, which had Pentecostal beliefs. She had prayed that God would lead her to the nearest church, that believed like she does, because after surgery on both shoulders, she could barely drive. Now she only had to drive ten miles to and from church.

He told her that her not going to the Baptist Church was "childish ignorance". He has become more and more confused and delusional. A few days ago he bet her $500,000.00 that their money market account percentage was higher than the checking account percentage. So, she got the bank statements and proved to him that he was wrong. She told him that he owed her that $500K, because he lost the bet. He said "oh, I said if I had it". She reminded him, that he did not say that, and he does have it. Never the less, he would not talk about it, anymore.

During 2014 & 2015, Beulah had frequent visits to a Urologist for multiple Urinary and Female problems. He kept her on so many medications and argued with her when she told him she had allergic reactions to some of them. He had a Doctor office in one side of his building and a Lawyer office in the other. She was sure that he was a Defense Lawyer, because of the way he argued about everything. He kept her with so many medications, that she never heard the like. She finally cancelled three future appointments and refused to go back to him. She realized that she was better off on her own.

Beulah's third granddaughter was born 2/2015. She had black eyes and hair. She is very smart and beautiful. She is the daughter of Beulah's oldest grandchild. Also, her first great grandson was born 12/16 to her second granddaughter. It was so exciting to finally have a boy in the family.

During 2015 Beulah realized that Heth's mental illness had increased to the point that he was "Borderline". He had become almost impossible to live with and began to curse her in his rages. He was continuously verbally and physically abusive. Strange thing. He was now very active and show–off in church. He was a Musician (played the guitar, and singing), assistant Sunday School Teacher, a deacon, and showed signs of an extravert, which was so out of character for him. He was Mr. Famous/Popular, and worked for benefits, for the church.

For sixty-five years he chauffeured the "Shiloam Sisters" to do music programs over North Georgia and South Carolina. They are disabled now, so he has inherited the "spotlight", mixing in some Country and Contemporary music with the Gospel.

She began to have trembling in the left side of her face, from playing the Violin. The doctors told her that she was having Mini Strokes. She had to give up playing string instruments in 2015. She had given up playing the piano and organ in 2012, because of Arthritis in her shoulders, arms, hands and fingers. She quit going to Gospel Music, Country and Bluegrass functions, because it was too emotional for her, that she could not perform

All that did not stop him. He began to search for every group, who would let him play guitar with them. He just went without her. It did not bother him. He became a real "blooming idiot", who just bloomed all the time. After three years he began to have problems with his back, and right leg, from carrying his guitar case against that leg and hip. He has two Hernias and shoulder pains, but he still would not give it up. He also found out that he has a Mass Tumor on his right kidney, but it is benign. His brother has one on his kidney, and his mother died from a Tumor on her kidney that was Cancer.

Farris had her third Pacemaker put in. The doctor told her that this would be her last one. Beulah's doctor said they only last six years. Beulah wonders if that means Farris will live only six more years. Tomorrow is not a given.

In May Heth carried his younger sister to Camp in west Georgia for four days. They both are wild about traveling, and talk about where they can plan to go next, each time they talk to each other. She spends money like she is a millionaire. He is a stingy stooge, and is a millionaire. She was manager of a department store for twenty-eight years. This is the third year they have gone camping together and stayed in Beulah and Heth's camper. They play poker, for "change" (small money), at night, until midnight. They have gone on fishing trips for several days, and stayed in Beulah and Heth's Condo's for a week at a time. They love having fun, do not know the difference between joy and happiness, and just want, want, want, to get, get, get. They are never full or have enough.

In October he carried his younger sister, brother and his wife up to the Condo in the Tennessee Mountains for a week. They all three go to Flea Markets like they are going out of style.

During Beulah's whole life, she had not been cursed by anyone. However, Heth began to curse her. In April 2016, Heth was planning another trip, with his sister, and Beulah did not like it. He cursed her and shouted "you will not stop me from doing what I want to do". Fine the Lord had already showed her that she could live by any of his rules. He yelled that he would pay for a sitter to stay with her. Therefore, when he goes, she writes her a check for half of the fees, vehicle expenses, and meals, plus $100.00 per day for a personal sitter. He has no way of knowing who might or might not sit with her. Beulah had become physically unable to travel long trips.

Heth failed to put rat poison in the camper, when he winterized it. Rats got into it, and made a 10" x 12" bed between the mattress and comforter, about middle of the bed. They ate the top of the fabric. He spent three days upholstery, shampooing the mattress, washing and mending the cover and comforter, patching the holes, and cleaning out the rat beds.

Heth scraped flaked paint off of the front cement porch swept it into the flower beds around the porch, after Beulah had just paid someone to clean out the flower beds, the week before.

Regarding Beulah's relationship with her parents, and husband, the diagnosis which emerged only a few years ago, "Reactive Attachment Disorder", might explain some of Beulah's feelings of being neglected and unloved. At least it cannot be totally ruled out.

This morning she finished breakfast, and reached for her medical bill to write a check, and it was not where she had her bills stacked. Heth denied ever touching any of them. Knowing him she was sure that he had miss placed it. She could tell that he had been through the bills, because he never puts things back like she has them. She sat down to her desk to work and both of her ball point pens were gone. He denied touching them.

What to do? She read her bible for a while, then decided to go to the bedroom to do some work. He was sitting with the metal file drawer pulled all the way out, with his chair in front of it blocking the door way to the bedroom. So, she decided to go through the files to see if she had mistakenly filed that medical bill. No. She thought that she would go on line and print out the bill, but it had been deleted. Therefore, she went back through the bills and found it stuck in a larger envelop with an Insurance bill. She went to look for the Pens, and found one in his desk, and the other on his dresser, just as she expected. This is a typical morning for her. He keeps her upset every day doing stupid things, and denying them. He never owns up to things which he has done.

You would not believe the things he keeps in their refrigerator: six bottles of Prostrate medicine (in a Pharmacy bag), three wet paint brushes wrapped in old newspapers, then in plastic grocery bags, his hot peppers, his jams of several sorts, gobs of grapes, apples, and other fruits (all of which Beulah does not eat). For breakfast he eats a mixture of four kinds of cereals in a bowl soaked in milk, with Raisins, Craisins, Prunes, and sliced fruit. He eats a desert after every meal, grapes and apples, or other fruits. He is a Diabetic and is not suppose to eat sweets. He has to have something to read while he eats. If there is no mail to look through, magazines, or newspapers to read, he will hunt something to read.

Beulah said when she moved back to her home place in Georgia, that next time she moved she was going up. She is enjoying her life on the same farm where she was raised. Early in the morning she reads her Bible, then documents in her Diary, the events of yesterday. She is trying to practice being more kind to Heth. She is resentfully learning to be patient and understanding, as well as be more cautiously forgiving.

It is not unusual to see up to fifteen Deer, at one time, in the field behind the kitchen. Yesterday she saw a mama Turkey, with eight of her little "bitties" crossing the road, in front of the house.

Here it is Fall of the year, again. In spite of Beulah's physical ailments, and handicaps, she has in the past week vacuumed, dusted, and sprayed for spiders, in one third of her Art Studio, swept two porches, swept and cleaned off the patio, table, and yard chairs, washed four loads of clothes, made a Crock Pot full of Brunswick Stew, not to mention did secretarial work on the computer, filing, bookwork, and other household choirs. Not bad for an eighty-three year old lady.

Heth is still painting the trim of the house, and picking up Pecans from their Orchard. Dennis calls daily and drops by about twice a week. On Saturday mornings, he and his wife walk the path around the sixteen acre farm, and they speak. This weekend the four of them are traveling about one and a half hours to their adopted son Wally Park's place on the lake, for his son's wedding.

Since Daniel retired from the Army, after thirty-three years, things have been better as far as Beulah and Heth's relationship. Daniel purchased the Shiloam house and farm. Therefore, he lives next door. He visits or calls every day. He is a mentor and inspiration for Heth. Daniel is such a genius. He stops by and fixes the computers for his parents, with "no charge". Therefore, when he needs help, they do things for him. His dad takes his tractor and does work for him on his farm, with "no charge".

It has been hard living "a day's drive" from their two sons, their grandchildren and their great grandchildren. Having one next door, now, is like a ray of "Sunshine". When his children and grands come to visit, Beulah and Heth get to be part of the family.

They do enjoy being close to their siblings, nieces, and nephews. The family gets together at Beulah's on holidays.

Three weeks ago, Beulah had surgery for Squamish Cell Carcenomas, on her left temple. It left a two inch scar.

Heth got angry recently, because she showed him a card which the Electric Company advertised "faster internet service" for only $15.00 more each month, than what they currently pay. He said "that would be $600.00 a year, and we are not doing it." She replied "well what if I do it" He said "then you will pay for it." She said "I will out of our joint account, because you need it too." He said that he did not need it, that she was the one who is impatient. She reminded him, that he made a new rule for the house hold, March 13, this year "I will do what I want to do, and you cannot stop me." She told him that she talked to God about that, and God told her that "it is O.K. for her to live by his rules." He told her "you need to get your ass on top of your head." She calmly said "Wow, that sounds just like a deacon or preacher." He is a deacon, a Sunday school teacher, and big church worker. Ever since that he has been so humble and sweet. He carried her shopping on Black Friday and bought her a lot of new clothes. "Whew"!!

Printed in the United States
By Bookmasters